THE RHYTHM CHANGES GUIDE

Exercises
Concepts
Practice Strategies
Etudes

LUKAS GABRIC

Sher Music Co.

PLAY-ALONG TRACKS

The play-along tracks that accompany this book are available for free download at www.shermusic.com. Just go to the "CD Downloads" tab at the top of our home page.

Rhythm section:

Manuel Weyand – Drums

Jazz drummer Manuel Weyand has performed internationally with a myriad of renown artists such as Danny Grissett, Jon Gordon, Julian Shore, Benny Benack, Sam Dillon, Lukas Gabric, Chad LB, Randy Johnston, Bjorn Solli, etc. in venues and festivals such as Smoke Jazz Club NYC, Blue Note NYC, Mr Kelly's Osaka, Porgy and Bess Vienna, Jarasum Jazz Festival, The Fringe Festival etc.

He holds a Master of Music from the Manhattan School of Music and currently serves as Professor of Applied Music at the Paekche Institute of the Arts.

Paul Kirby – Piano

Paul Kirby (born 1981) is a pianist, composer and arranger, originally from Edinburgh, UK. He has performed with some of the top names in jazz including Herb Geller, Jesse Davis, Steve Grossman, Jim Snidero, Billy Hart, Tim Armacost, Peter King, Vincent Herring, Eric Alexander, vocalist Kenny Washington and Ken Peplowski amongst many others. He has performed on TV and Radio many times in Europe (BBC/UK, BR/Germany, etc) and South Korea (KBS, EBS, etc).

Daeho Kim – Bass

Seoul native Daeho Kim is one of the busiest bassists on the Korean jazz scene. He was born in 1984 and has gathered extensive experience in the classical and pop genres during his formative years. He is an alumnus of Kyunghee University where he majored in postmodern music. It is not hard to find his name in many festival, concert, and jazz club programs all over South Korea. The recording of his duo project entitled, "Acousticology," was released in 2015. He is widely known as a tremendously reliable sideman, bandleader, and capable arranger. Among his performance credits he can cite collaborations with the two American alto saxophone giants Jesse Davis and Vincent Herring.

YongMun Lee - Recording Engineer

Cover and Interior Design: Richell Balansag

©2020 Sher Music Co., www.shermusic.com
All Rights Reserved. No part of this book may be reproduced
in any form without written permission from the publisher.
ISBN - 978-0-9976617-6-7

CONTENTS

Introduction 6

List of Rhythm Changes Contrafacts 7

How to Use this Book 9

Rhythm Changes – Harmonic Structure 10
    Units A, B, & A' In Rhythm Changes 12
    Structural Levels 13
    Sources Of Chromaticism 13
    The Three Levels 14
    Background Level 15
    Foreground Level 18
    Predominant Chords 18
    Secondary Dominant Chords 19
    Passing Diminished Chords 19
    Related Chords 19

Harmonic Variations Of The A Section: Examples From The Masters ... 21
    How to Practice the Loops 24

Harmonic Variations of Unit A 26
    Harmonic Variations of the first 4-measure segment of the A section ... 28
        Circle of Fifths & Half Steps 28
        Tritone Substitution 28
        Examples From The Masters 28
        Whole Steps 32
        Minor Thirds 33
        Major Thirds 34

Harmonic Variations of Unit B 35
Harmonic Variations of Unit B: Examples from the Masters 36

Harmonic Variations Spanning the Entire A Section 38
Half steps 38
Whole Steps 40
Minor Thirds 41
Major Thirds 42

Harmonic Variations of the Bridge (B Section) 43
Examples From The Masters: Bridge 44

Target Notes and Guide Tone Lines 47
Review Of Ornamental Notes 47
Use Of Ornamental Notes: Examples From The Masters 48
Target Note Lines Consisting of Thirds 49
Target Note Lines Consisting of Fifths 50
Target Note Lines Consisting of Sevenths 51
Guide Tone Lines 52
Rules for Constructing Guide Tone Lines 52
Guide Tone Line from 3rd of the First Chord 52

Diatonic Playing 53
Guide Tone Lines with a Schenkerian Approach 53
Schenker and his Perspective 53
How to Read the Graphs & Examples 54
Did the Masters Really Know that and Think Like that? 54
Guide Line – Schenkerian Approach 54
Example 1 – Schenkerian 5-Descent 54
Example 2 – Schenkerian 5-Descent 56
Example 3 – Schenkerian 5-Descent with Initial Ascent 57
Example 4 – Schenkerian 3-Descent 58
Register Transfer & Octave Equivalence 58
Schenkerian Lines: Examples From The Masters 59

Other Diatonic Techniques 61
Triads 61
Embellishing Triads: Examples From The Masters 61
Triadic Embellishments: Exercises Derived From The Masters 63
Sequences: Examples From the Masters 64
Sequence Exercises 66
Use Of The Blues Scale: Examples From The Masters 67
Pentatonic Scales 68

Etudes 70
Etude 1 "Five" 70
Etude 2 "Common Ground" 70
Etude 3 "Four" 71
Etude 4 "Combination" 71
Etude 5 "Follow The Line" 71
Etude 6 "Big Picture" 71
Etude 7 "Upside Down" 71
Etude 8 "Options" 72
Etude 9 "Chicago" 72
Etude 10 "Big Bird" 72
Etude 11 "For Vic" 72
Etude 12 "Excursion" 72
Etude 13 "Steppin' Down" 73
Etude 14 "Mirror Image" 73
Etude 15 "Express Train" 73
Etude 16 "Big Red" 73
Etude 17 "The Patron" 73
Etude 18 "Trial and Error" 74
Etude 19 "Choices" 74
Etude 20 "Little Bird" 74

Recordings 95

**PDF versions of etudes in Eb, Bb, and Bass Clef available
for free download at www.shermusic.com**

INTRODUCTION

The rhythm changes progression, famously derived from George Gershwin's song "I Got Rhythm," is arguably one of the most important vehicles in jazz. The song's harmonic progression and 32-bar AABA form, have been used for countless contrafacts throughout jazz history. Due to its importance, many teachers recommend the mastery of rhythm changes in every key.

The popularity of rhythm changes is likely based on the various progressions that occur within the tune. The same progressions are found in almost every jazz standard, such as the tonicization of IVmaj^7, a move from IVmaj^7 to iv^6 ($\flat$VII^7 or $\sharp$iv$^\circ$), I-VI^7-ii^7-V^7 turnarounds, or chains of secondary dominants. In rhythm changes all these progressions occur in relatively rapid succession. There are seemingly countless possibilities for harmonic variations of the rhythm changes progression.

Rhythm changes has become somewhat of a testing ground for improvisers. Advanced jazz performers are expected to demonstrate their knowledge of the tradition when performing rhythm changes.

This book is aimed at presenting the dedicated musician with a variety of material derived from the tradition as well as strategies to learn and apply it effectively and creatively. Some of the most important melodic and harmonic devices from the rhythm changes tradition were used to compose the twenty etudes in the last section of the book.

LIST OF RHYTHM CHANGES CONTRAFACTS

- "Anthropology / Thriving on a Riff" (C. Parker & D. Gillespie)
- "Apple Jump" (D. Gordon)
- "Blue's Theme" (B. Mitchell)
- "The Bridge" (S. Rollins)
- "C.T.A." (J. Heath)
- "Celerity" (C. Parker)
- "Chasin' the Bird" (C. Parker)
- "Chasm" (J. Adderley)
- "Chippie" (O. Coleman)
- "Chronology" (O. Coleman)
- "Constellation" (C. Parker)
- "Cottontail" (D. Ellington)
- "Crazeology" (B. Harris)
- "Dexterity" (C. Parker)
- "Dizzy Atmosphere" (D. Gillespie)
- "Don't Be That Way" (B. Goodman, E. Sampson, M. Parish)
- "The Eternal Triangle" (S. Stitt)
- "Tricotism" (O. Pettiford)
- "Fingers" (T. Jones)
- "Finger Poppin'" (H. Silver)
- "Flintstones Theme" (H. Curtin)
- "Fungi Mama" (B. Mitchell)
- "Good Bait" (T. Dameron)
- "Jay Bird" (J.J. Johnson)
- "Jay Jay" (J.J. Johnson)
- "Lester Leaps In" (L. Young)
- "Lo Joe" (G. Coleman)
- "Moose the Mooche" (C. Parker)

- "Nutty" (T. Monk)
- "Oleo" (S. Rollins)
- "An Oscar for Treadwell" (C. Parker)
- "Passport" (C. Parker)
- "Rhythm-a-Ning" (T. Monk)
- "Room 608" (H. Silver)
- "Salt Peanuts" (D. Gillespie)
- "Second Balcony Jump" (B. Eckstine & G. Valentine)
- "Seven, Come Eleven" (C. Christian & B. Goodman)
- "Steeplechase" (C. Parker)
- "Straight Ahead" (K. Dorham)
- "Suspone" (M. Stern)
- "The Theme" (M. Davis)
- "Tippin'" (H. Silver)
- "Wail" (B. Powell)
- "Webb City" (B. Powell)
- "Wee" (D. Gillespie)
- "Wells Fargo" (W. Harden)

_____
_____
_____
_____
_____
_____

*This is just a selection of contrafacts that were inspired by rhythm changes. Use the empty lines for additional contrafacts you find.

HOW TO USE THIS BOOK

1. Always practice with a reference to metronomic time
2. Start slowly and increase the tempo
3. Isolate passages that you have difficulties with
4. Use the etudes for your auditions, juries, and competitions
5. Play the exercises and etudes with your friends or with a play along
6. Record yourself playing the exercises and etudes
7. Analyze the etudes
8. Play the exercises and etudes in different keys
9. Take little segments you like and practice them through the keys at various tempos
10. Write your own etudes over the given chord progressions
11. Apply the various practice strategies to the harmonic loops
12. Use the etudes to improve and develop your:
    - Reading
    - Articulation
    - Instrumental Technique
    - Familiarity with the jazz language & knowledge of the tradition
    - Time feel
    - Transposition
    - Intonation
    - Memorization
    - Compositional and Improvisational understanding
    - Knowledge and Flexibility of Harmony

RHYTHM CHANGES – HARMONIC STRUCTURE

Rhythm changes follows a 32-bar AABA form with specific chords (see page 12). Gershwin's original song includes a tag, which is added to the last A section that is generally left out in contrafacts.

The A sections consist of two different harmonic units. Unit A occurs three times while unit B happens only once in every A section.

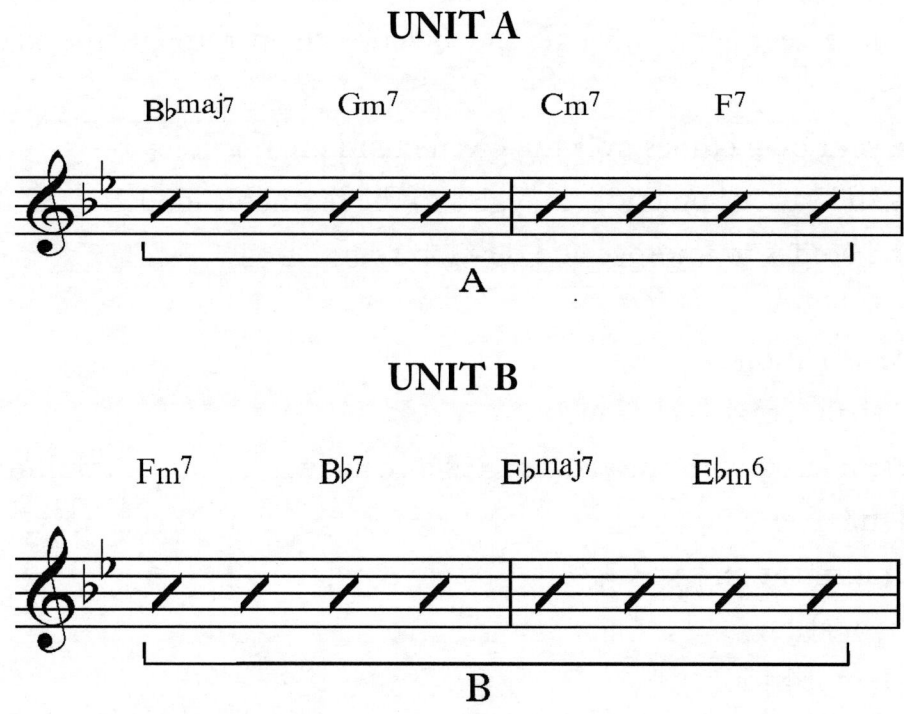

Unit B is part of the A section and not to be confused with the bridge, which is also designated as "B"

The second A section of rhythm changes is an exception. Its final two measures are basically just two bars of the tonic chord. This unit is labeled as A'.

UNIT A'

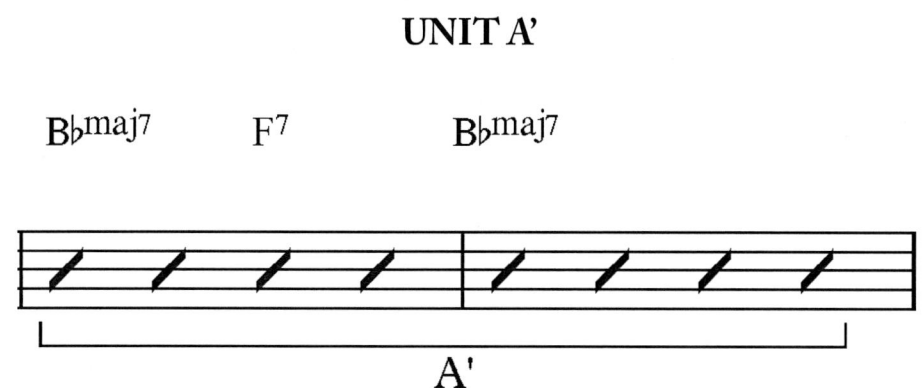

Due to the inventiveness of the jazz legends, many harmonic variations of these two-bar units have been absorbed into the jazz tradition. There are also many harmonic variations that span four-measure subsections, or even entire A sections. The same applies to the B section. Knowing the structure of the piece helps you to practice it and play with more flexibility.

UNITS A, B, & A' IN RHYTHM CHANGES

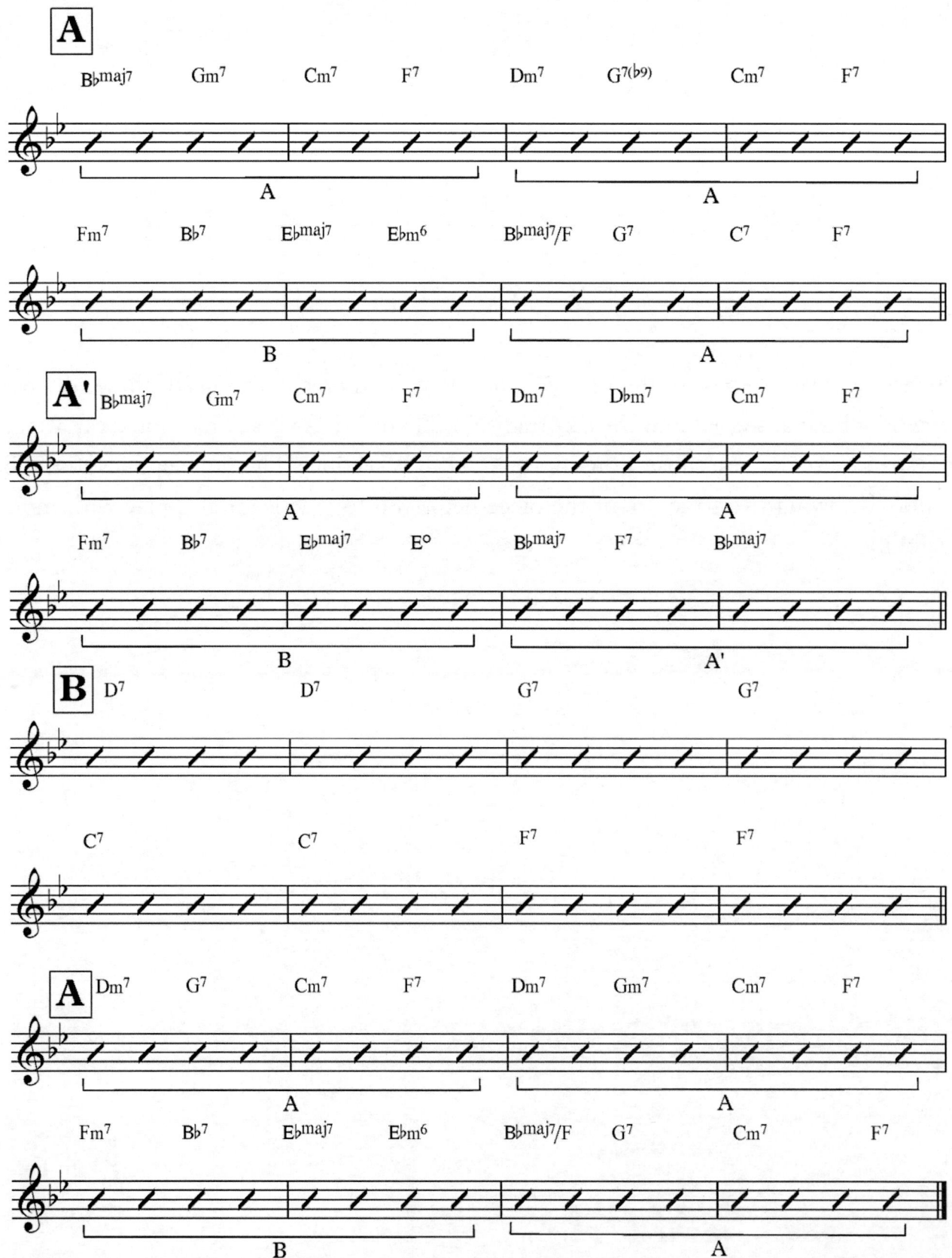

STRUCTURAL LEVELS

As in ordinary life, we make discoveries by looking at things through a microscope and by viewing satellite images. The same can be done with jazz standards. Once we are familiar with the different zoomed-in or zoomed-out perspectives of a tune, we can take advantage of it in our playing. To fully understand a piece and its harmonic design it is very helpful to be aware of its "big picture" and its "microscopic level."

If we apply the satellite image approach to the A sections of rhythm changes, we find that we are dealing with a prolonged tonic chord. In other words, the whole A section is simply B♭ major in the original key. Similarly, the B section can be seen as a trip to the dominant chord. This satellite image view is called "background-level."

Only the most important harmonic events matter at the background level – everything else is considered ornamental and left out. The background level is the most zoomed-out structural level. When you hear Sonny Rollins, John Coltrane, or Sonny Stitt only using the B♭ major scale in an A section, they are taking advantage of the background level perspective.

Most of the solos of the masters consist of a well-balanced mix of diatonic (=in the key) melodies that include some well-chosen chromaticism (=not in the key).

SOURCES OF CHROMATICISM

Chromaticism usually stems from superimposed secondary dominant chords, chordal extensions, various dominant scales, passing diminished chords, harmonic superimpositions, and embellishments of diatonic material, such as the tonic triad.

Beside the background level, we can also look at a tune from a middle ground view and apply a foreground perspective. Awareness of the three different harmonic structural levels enables us to use various strategies to play with.

THE THREE LEVELS

Foreground Level

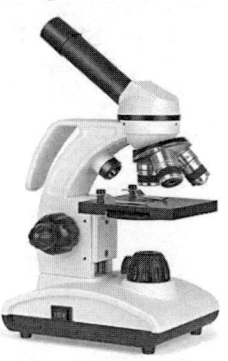

View through Microscope

Middle Ground Level

View from a tall building

Background level

Satellite Image

THE RHYTHM CHANGES GUIDE

BACKGROUND LEVEL

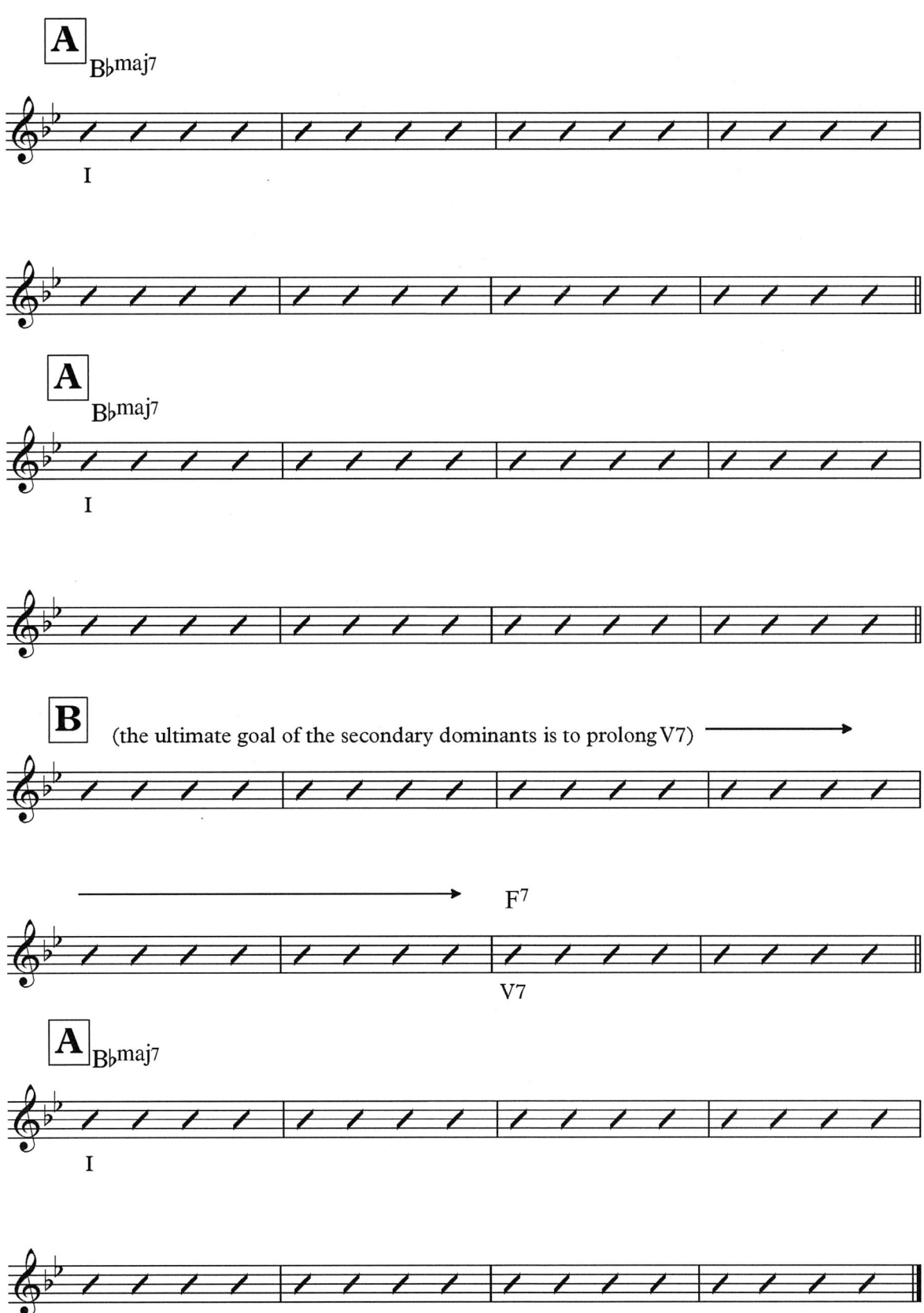

Two important characteristics of the background level

1) The A sections are sustained tonic chords
2) The B section is essentially a journey to V

MIDDLE GROUND LEVEL

Tonic (I) and dominant (V^7) chords alternate every measure for the first four bars and the final two measures of each A section.

At the harmonic middle ground level, the A sections of the rhythm changes progression also includes an important move to IV in the 6th, 14th, and 30th measures of the form.

A♭ is an essential non-diatonic pitch, which signals the move to IV within the A section.

If an improviser only plays notes of the B♭ major scale but includes an A♭ in the fifth measure of the A section, the player is using the middle ground level.

Two important characteristics of the middle ground level

1) I and V^7 chords switch off in the first four, and last two measures of the A section
2) Move to IV in the fifth and sixth measure of the A section
3) The bridge consists of four dominant chords that proceed through the circle of fifths

THE RHYTHM CHANGES GUIDE
(Playlist Track 1)

Rhythm Changes - Middle ground level

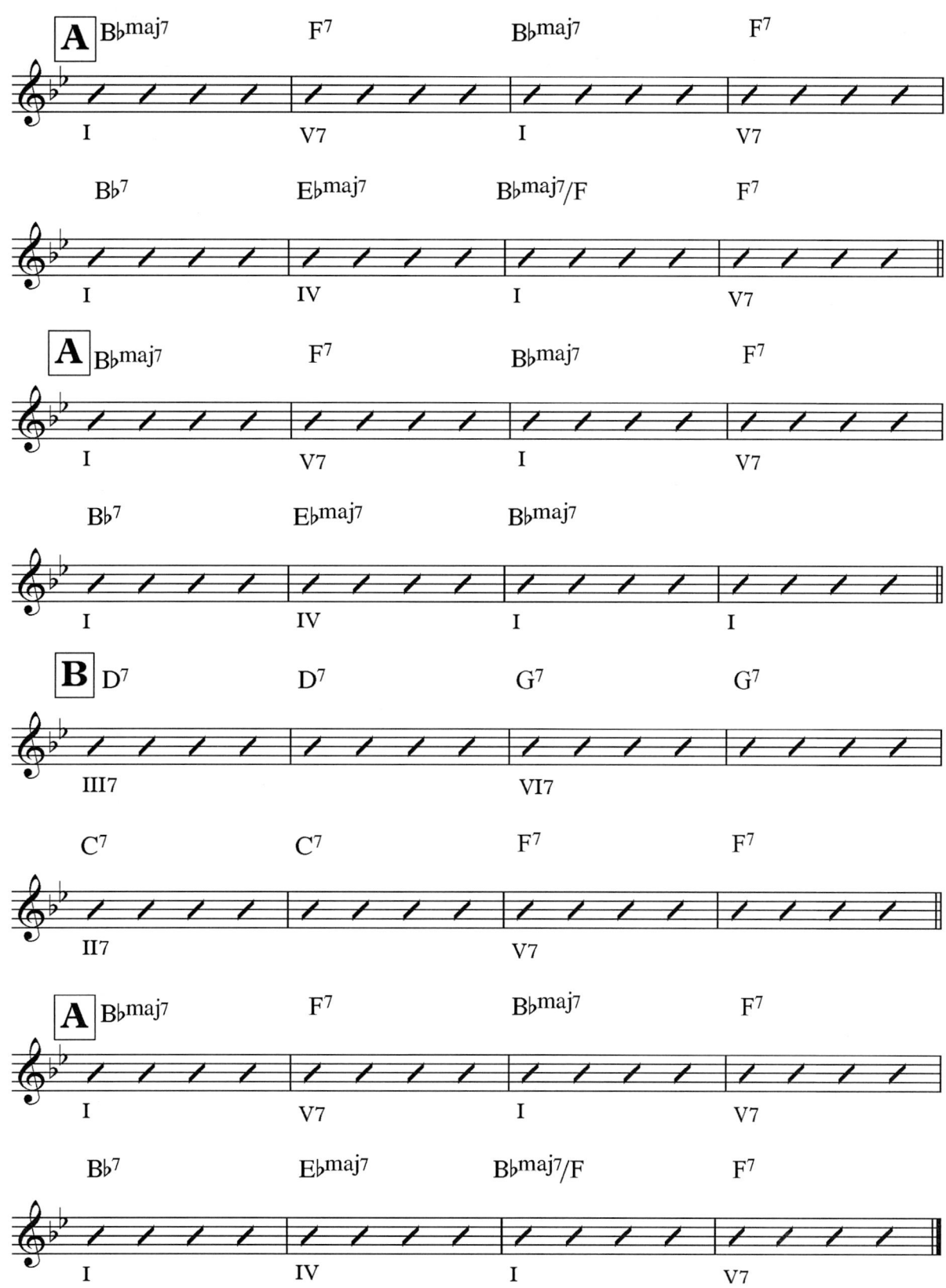

FOREGROUND LEVEL

At the foreground level (see page 10) many chords are added that are not included in the middle ground and background levels. When we hear someone say that someone is "nailing the changes" or "spelling it out," they mean that the player is outlining the foreground level chords very well.

Keep in mind that rhythm sections usually play at the foreground level, but the middle ground and background levels are still always there. The higher levels are just hidden beneath the denser foreground harmonies.

The following are some of the chords that are added at the foreground level.

PREDOMINANT CHORDS

These are chords that come before the dominant chord of the key or key area. There are different kinds of predominant chords.

ii^7

The most commonly used predominant chord in jazz is the ii^7 chord. It is part of the ii-V-I progression that is built into every jazz standard. Sometimes improvisers turn the ii7 chord into a II7 chord in the A sections of rhythm changes, making it a secondary dominant chord.

IV

In classical music, IV is the most commonly used predominant chord. It is also called the "subdominant" because it is a step below the dominant chord V. Others think that IV is called the subdominant because it is a fifth below the root – thus the sub-dominant = lower dominant. In any case, IV is below or "sub" the dominant chord of the key.

$$F\ (IV) \Rightarrow C\ (I) \Leftarrow G\ (V)$$

This view also neatly explains how IV can lead to I in a blues cadence (plagal or amen cadence).

SECONDARY DOMINANT CHORDS

All dominant chords but the V chord of a key or key area are considered secondary dominant chords.

II^7

This is a very common secondary dominant chord in jazz. It functions as V/V. ii^7 frequently occurs in between II^7 and V, as in the A section of "Take the A Train" and countless other examples.

VI^7

This is also a very common secondary dominant chord in jazz. It functions as V/ii or V/II^7.

PASSING DIMINISHED CHORDS

In most cases, passing diminished chords bridge two diatonic chords that are a whole step apart in rhythm changes. E.g. C#° can be placed between Cmaj^7 and Dm^7. In this example C#° acts like a rootless A$^{7♭9}$ chord leading to Dm^7.

The whole-half diminished scale is used for passing diminished chords in jazz.

RELATED CHORDS

In rhythm changes, related chords are used to keep the music moving forward and exciting. Always playing the I chord makes it seem like we want to end the piece before it's actually finished. Accordingly, **iii^7 often replaces Imaj^7.**

Related chords are used to keep the music moving:

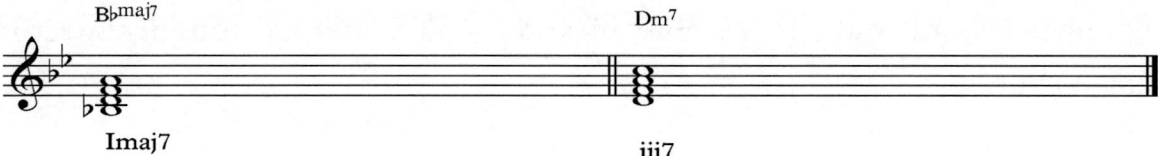

Imaj⁷ and iii⁷ share three identical pitches. In this example Bbmaj⁷ and Dm⁷ share the notes D, F, and A. Because of this, the two chords can replace each other.

If we include all chord extensions, as common in jazz, the two chords even share six pitches.:

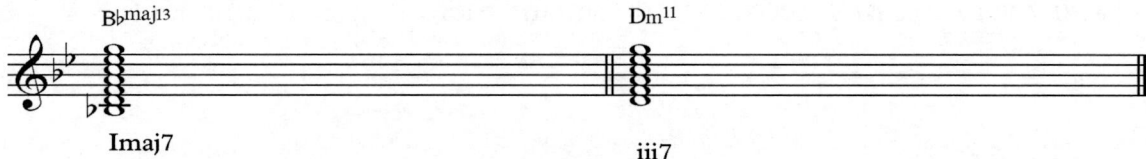

Since we are expected to outline the changes well, we have to become familiar with the foreground harmonies and their many variations.

HARMONIC VARIATIONS OF THE A SECTION: EXAMPLES FROM THE MASTERS

Legendary performers played with a great degree of flexibility and freely applied harmonic variations over the normal rhythm changes progression. This nimble approach is enabled though a deep knowledge of functional harmony and the jazz tradition. The ability to use alternative harmonic routes lets the performer play with variety, color, intrigue, and sophistication.

- Dexter Gordon on "Red Cross"

Here a biii^7 is placed between iii^7 and ii^7. Gordon also holds ii^7 into measure three and plays a vii°^{7}/V (E°) chord leading to V. The ordinary changes are completely reimagined within the first four measures of the A section.

- John Coltrane "Oleo"

Like Gordon, Coltrane superimposes a ♭iii⁷ chord and places it between iii⁷ and ii⁷ in the third measure.

- Charlie Parker "Thriving on a Riff"

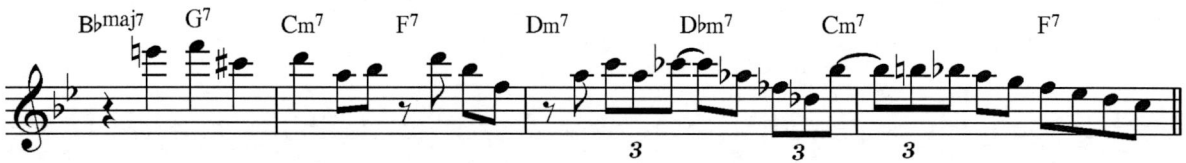

Parker also used this tactic and puts ♭iii7 between iii⁷ and ii⁷.

- Dexter Gordon "Second Balcony Jump"

Although this example stems from a Dexter Gordon solo, this harmonic progression is more typical of Coltrane. The B⁷ chord resolves to V/IV, B♭⁷.

- Dexter Gordon "Second Balcony Jump"

In this example, Gordon also places a ♭iii⁷ chord between iii⁷ and ii⁷ in the third measure.

- Dexter Gordon on "Red Cross"

Gordon descends in minor thirds for the first two measures of this example. He resolves back into iii⁷ or Imaj⁷.

- Hank Mobley "Room 608"

In the second measure of the A section, Mobley restates the first phrase up a semitone implying the tritone substitue of V.

- Michael Brecker "Anthropology"

In measures three and four of this A section, Brecker imposes two chromatically descending dominant chords that resolve to I⁷ (= B♭⁷ in the fifth measure).

- Sonny Rollins "Eternal Triangle"

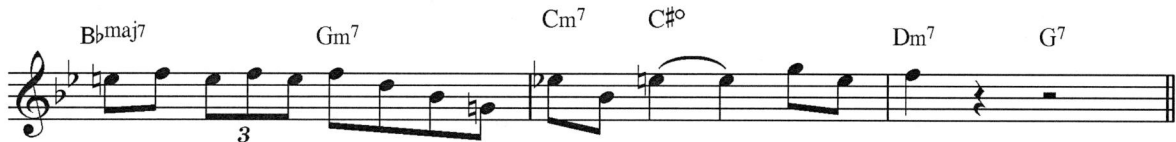

Here Rollins implies a ♯ii° chord in the second measure. Usually a V⁷ chord would be heard in its place. This is a great example of the use of a passing diminished chord.

- Sonny Stitt "Eternal Triangle"

Stitt implies vii°/iii in the same location as Rollins.

We see that the legends used a specific shared harmonic vocabulary. They speak the same language.

Many more variations of unit A exist within the A section. Since unit A makes up roughly 60% of rhythm changes, it is crucial to know the most common harmonic substitutions well.

On pages 26-27 several harmonic variations are listed as practice loops. Each loop begins with the normal harmony of unit A and is followed by a harmonic variation of unit A. The loops are designed to develop greater facility in applying harmonic variations and transitioning in and out of them. Each loop should be regarded as the first four measures of an A section.

Some of the loops are full-fledged harmonic variants and others merely contain different harmonic shadings - important sources for variety.

HOW TO PRACTICE THE LOOPS

1) Memorize them
2) Play the root of every chord in time with a metronome
3) Play every individual chord tone of every chord (e.g. play all thirds, then all fifths, etc. You can apply this to extensions as well)
4) Practice guide tone lines and target note lines though the loops
5) Arpeggiate each chord. You can do this in 4 ways:
    a. Ascend on all chords
    b. Descend on all chords
    c. Alternate between ascending and descending
    d. Alternate between descending and ascending
6) Play bass lines though the loops
7) Play the 24 permutations of the 1,2,3,5 though the loops
8) Play the 24 permutations of the 1,2,5,6 though the loops

9) Come up with your own tetrachord and practice its permutations though the progressions
10) Play a lick over every chord and adapt it as needed
11) Practice the loops in different keys
12) Write your own solos using the provided harmonies

HARMONIC VARIATIONS OF UNIT A

(Playlist Tracks 2-12)

THE RHYTHM CHANGES GUIDE
(Playlist Tracks 13-24)

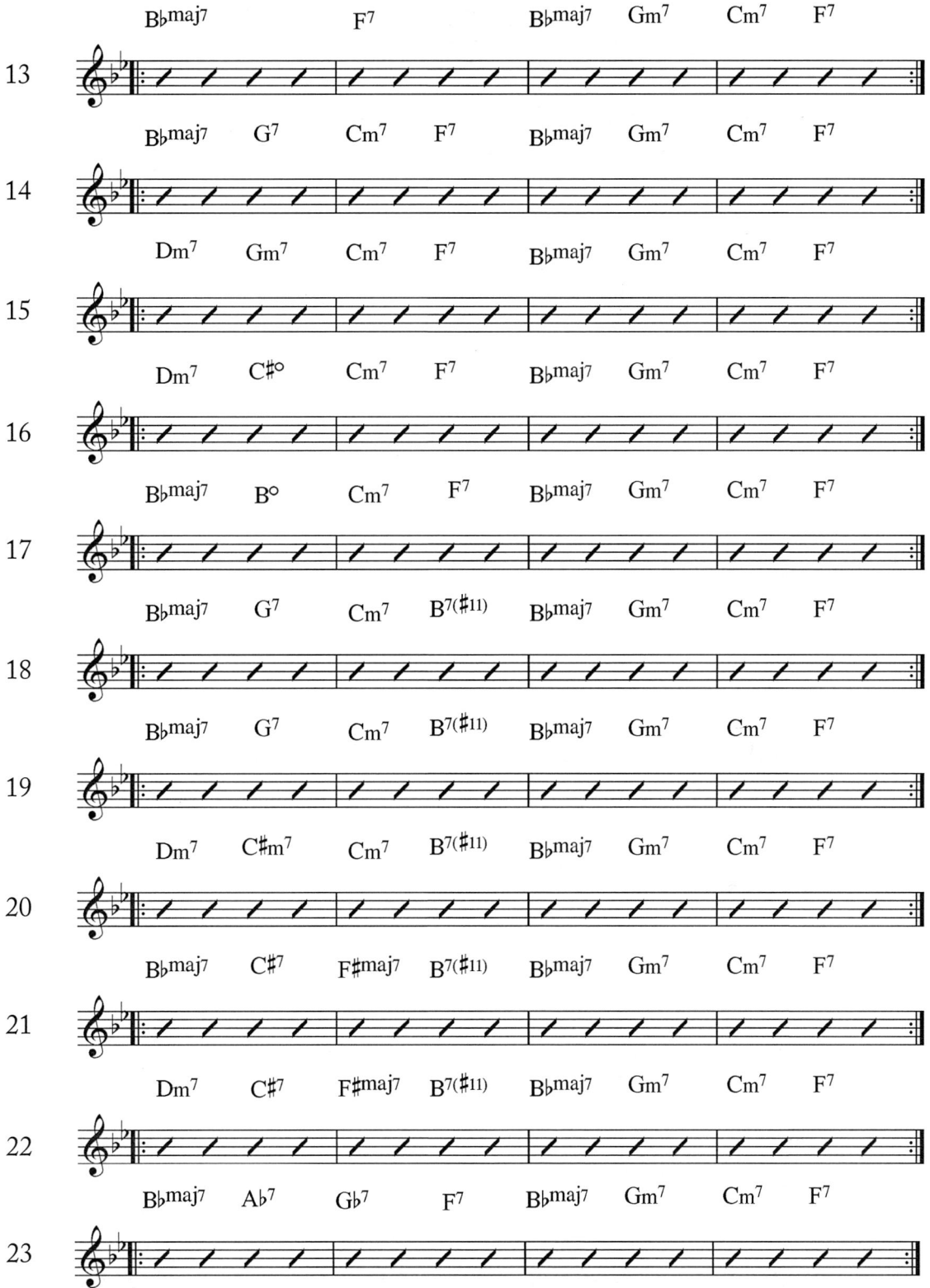

27

HARMONIC VARIATIONS OF THE FIRST 4-MEASURE SEGMENT OF THE A SECTION

CIRCLE OF FIFTHS & HALF STEPS

Many improvisers approach I^7 (B♭^{7}) or v^7 (Fm^7) in the fifth measure via a chain of secondary dominant chords. The resulting progression is a circle of fifths. Since dominant chords can be replaced with their tritone-substitutes, this progression can also be played as a chromatically descending progression of dominant chords.

TRITONE SUBSTITUTION

The fundamental idea behind tritone substitution is the fact that dominant seventh chords which are a tritone apart share the same thirds and sevenths.

Example:

The third and seventh of C^7 are E and B♭, which are enharmonically identical with the seventh and third of F♯^{7}. Accordingly, F♯^{7} can be substituted for C^7 and vice versa.

EXAMPLES FROM THE MASTERS

- Dexter Gordon on "Red Cross"

- Dexter Gordon on "Red Cross"

- Don Byas "I Got Rhythm"

In this example, Byas descends chromatically from II. This passage could also be seen as a circle of fifths progression in which every other chord is replaced by its tritone substitute – resulting in a chromatic progression.

- Don Byas "I Got Rhythm"

A variation of the chromatically descending harmonic superimposition.

- Don Byas "I Got Rhythm"

This is probably the earliest example of an implied circle of fifths progression in rhythm changes.

- Don Byas "I Got Rhythm"

Another variation of an implied circle of fifths progression.

- Dexter Gordon "Second Balcony Jump"

Ususally an implied circle of fifths is introduced in the first measure, but Gordon plays it in measure three in this example. The E chord in the last measure resolves up to the ii^7/IV in measure 5 (Fm^7). E is also the tritone substitue of B♭, which acts as the V/IV.

- Coltrane "The Theme" w/ Miles Davis

Here Coltrane uses a shortened form of Byas' chromatic superimpositon.

THE RHYTHM CHANGES GUIDE

(Playlist Tracks 24-31)

Variations for the entire first four-measure segment – circle of 4ths and half steps

Chromatically descending ii7-Vs

Chromatically ascending ii7-Vs

WHOLE STEPS

(Playlist Tracks 32-37)

Jimmy Heath uses the idea of descending whole steps in his contrafact "CTA."

Variations for the entire first four-measure segment – whole steps

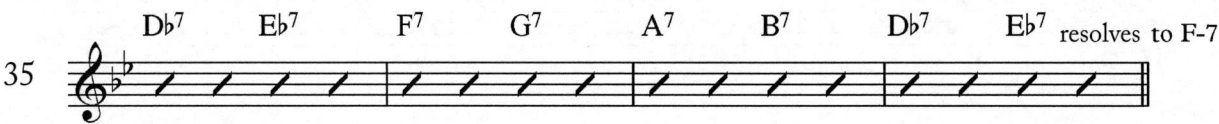

Descending ii7-Vs

MINOR THIRDS

(Playlist Tracks 38-41)

Variations for the entire first four-measure segment – minor thirds

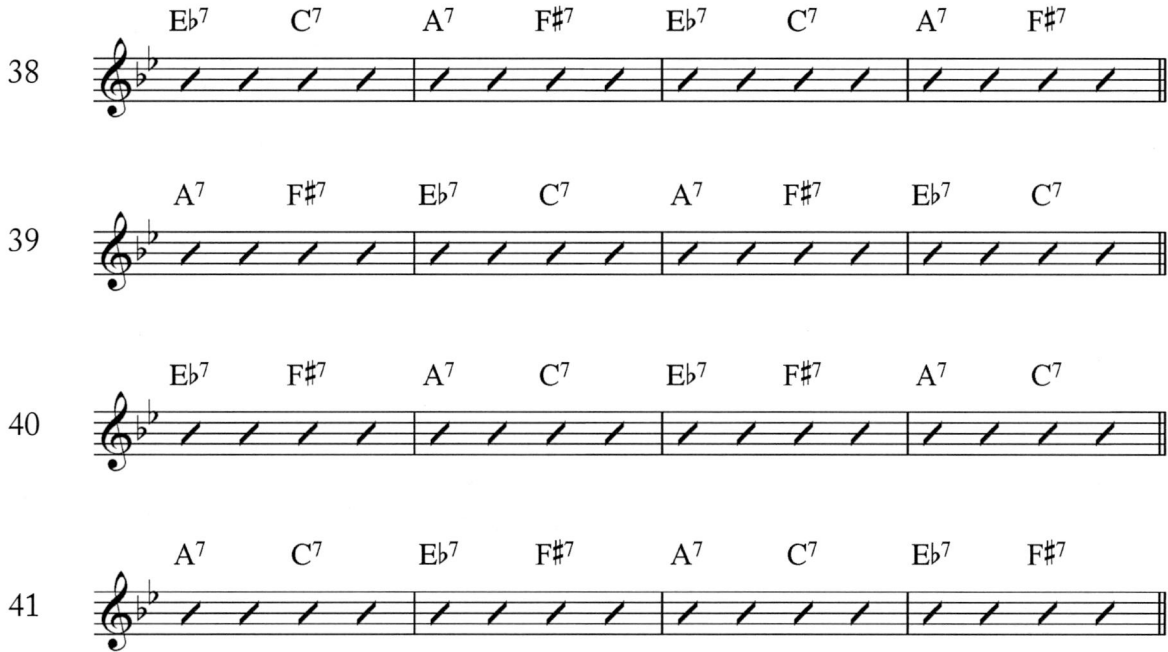

MAJOR THIRDS

(Playlist Tracks 42-45)

Variations for the entire first four-measure segment – minor thirds

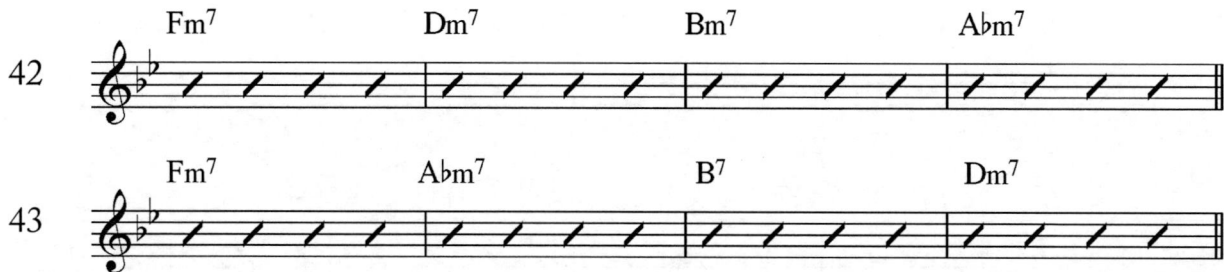

Variations for the entire first four-measure segment – major thirds

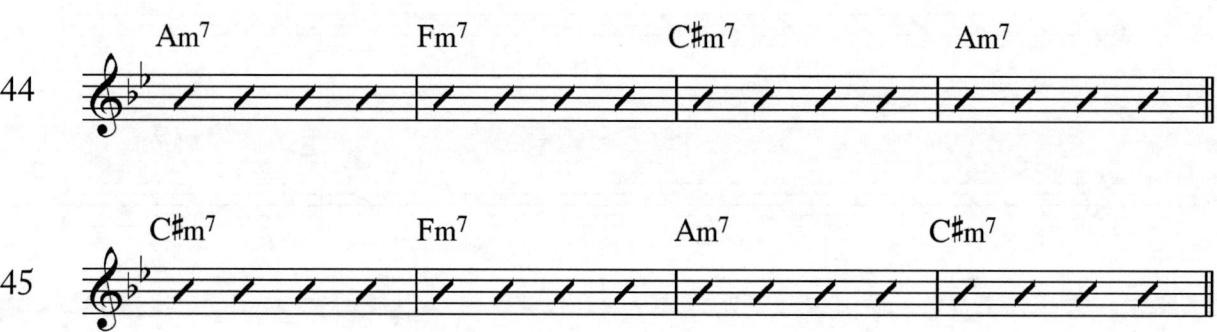

HARMONIC VARIATIONS OF UNIT B

(Playlist Tracks 46-55)

HARMONIC VARIATIONS OF UNIT B: EXAMPLES FROM THE MASTERS

- Sonny Rollins "Eternal Triangle"

In this example, Rollins implies a tritone substituted ii-V progression. He also displaces it rhythmically resulting in a 3/4 over 4/4 cross rhythm.

- Dexter Gordon "Second Balcony Jump"

Gordon uses a similar strategy in this example but without a cross rhythm.

- Sonny Rollins "Eternal Triangle"

E^7 replaces $B\flat^7$ in this example.

- Hank Mobley "Tenor Conclave"

D♭° is used as a passing diminished chord leading to iii. The chord could also be interpreted as ♯iv° moving to I/5. Usually iv or ♭VII⁷ would be used here.

- Don Byas "I Got Rhythm"

Historically, Byas used ♭iii° before Mobley in this specific place.

- Don Byas "I Got Rhythm"

In this example, Byas approaches ii/IV with the vii° chord E°/v.

HARMONIC VARIATIONS SPANNING THE ENTIRE A SECTION

HALF STEPS

(Playlist Tracks 56-59)

Harmonic Variations for first and third A sections

Ascending half steps

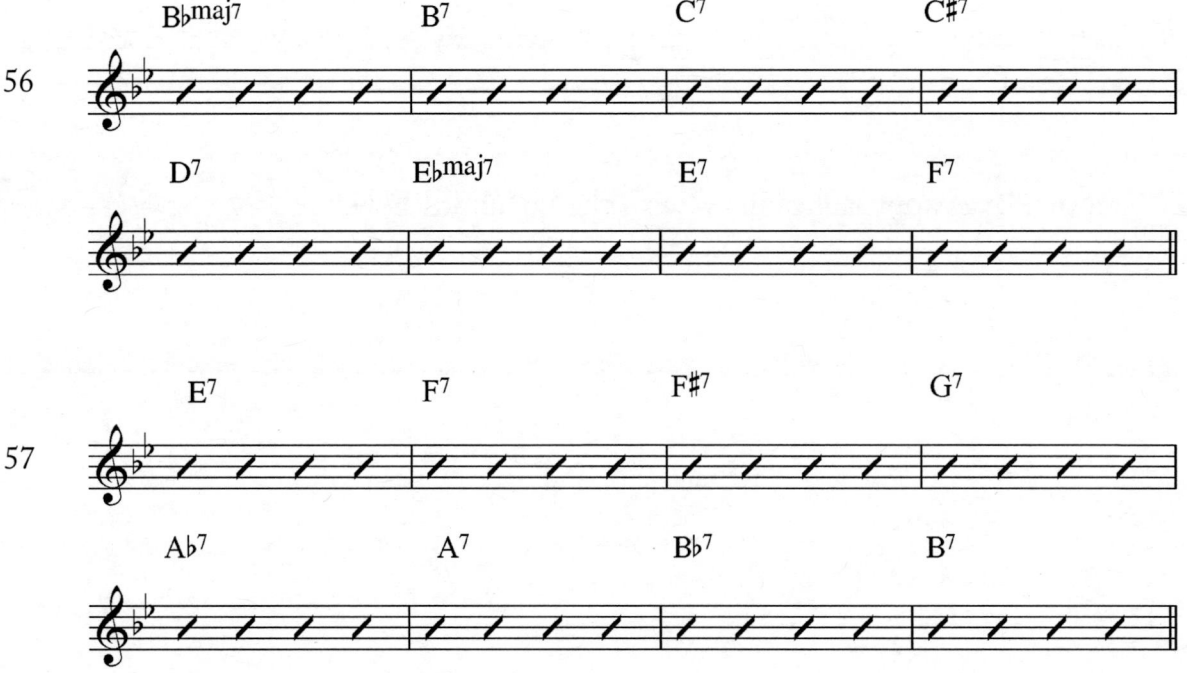

THE RHYTHM CHANGES GUIDE

Descending half steps

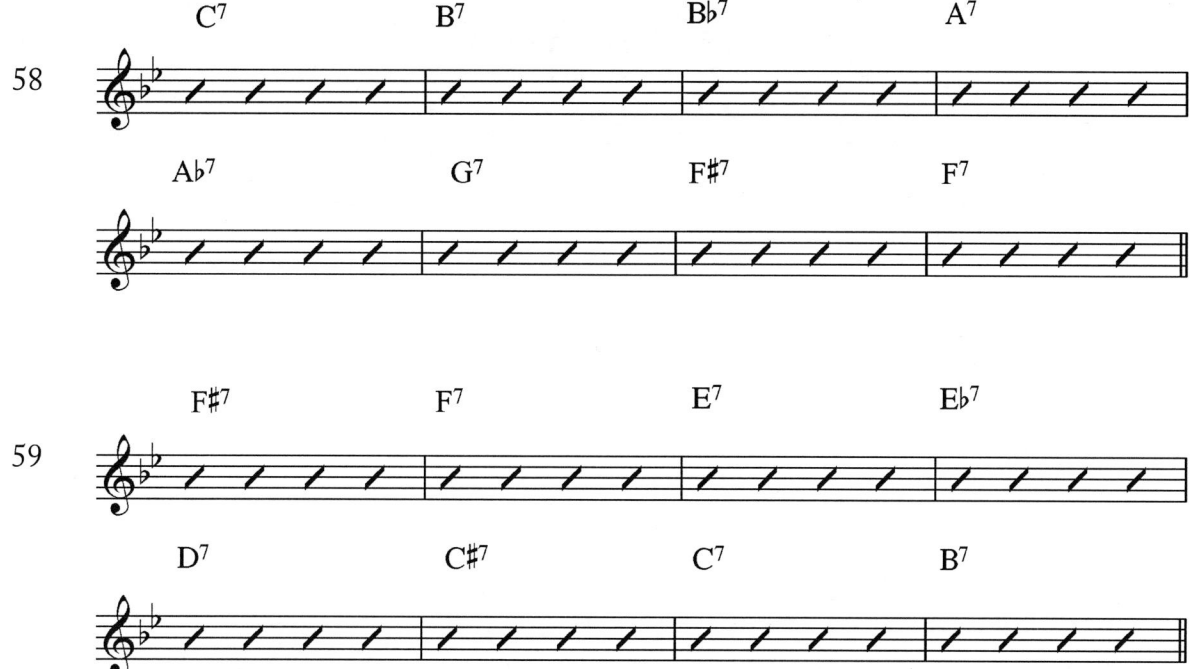

WHOLE STEPS

(Playlist Tracks 60-63)

Harmonic Variations for first and third A sections

Descending whole steps

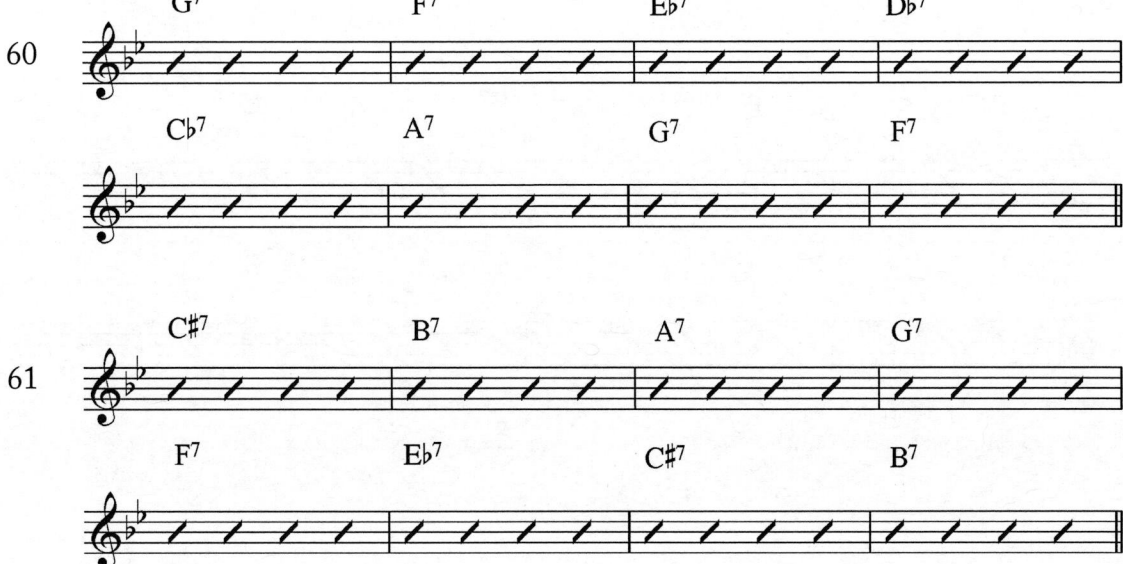

Ascending whole steps

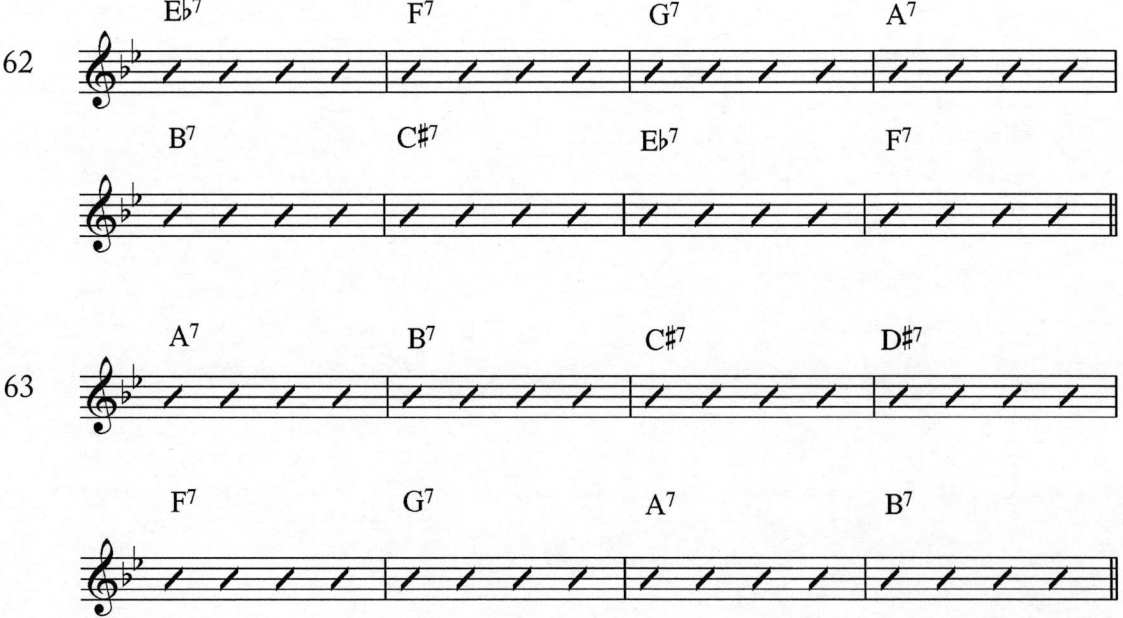

MINOR THIRDS

(Playlist Tracks 64-67)

Harmonic Variations for first and third A sections

Descending minor thirds

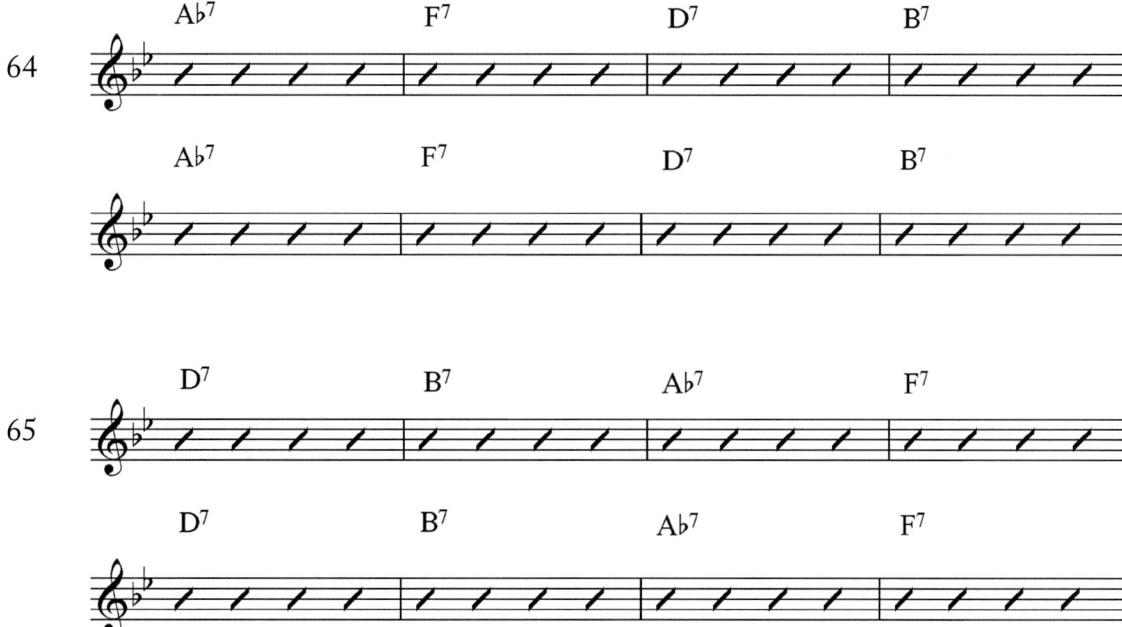

Ascending minor thirds

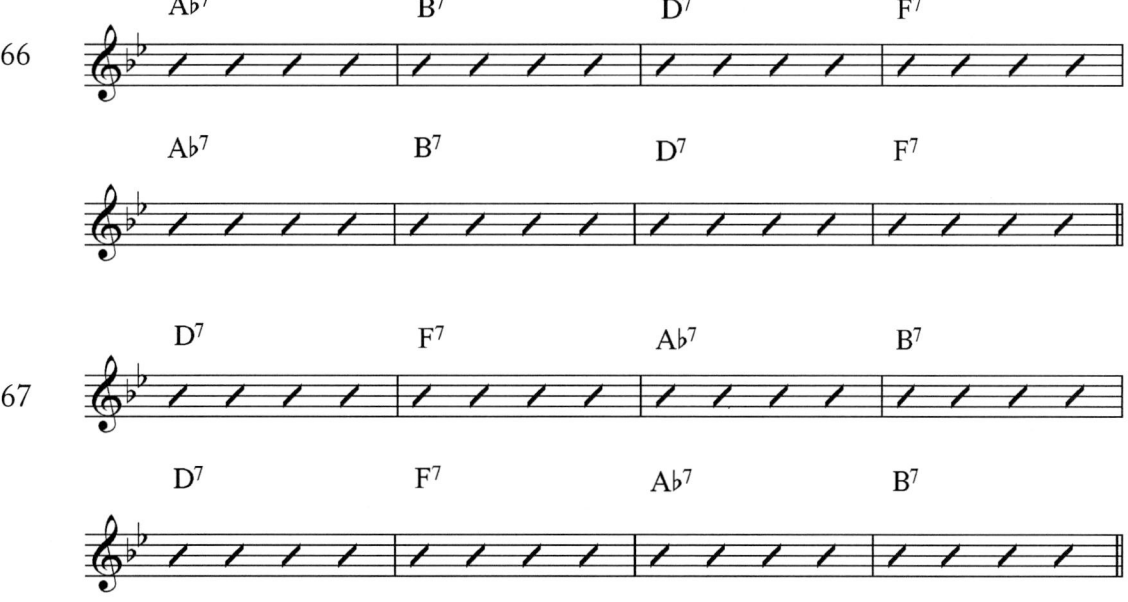

MAJOR THIRDS

(Playlist Tracks 68-71)

Harmonic Variations for first and third A sections

Descending major thirds

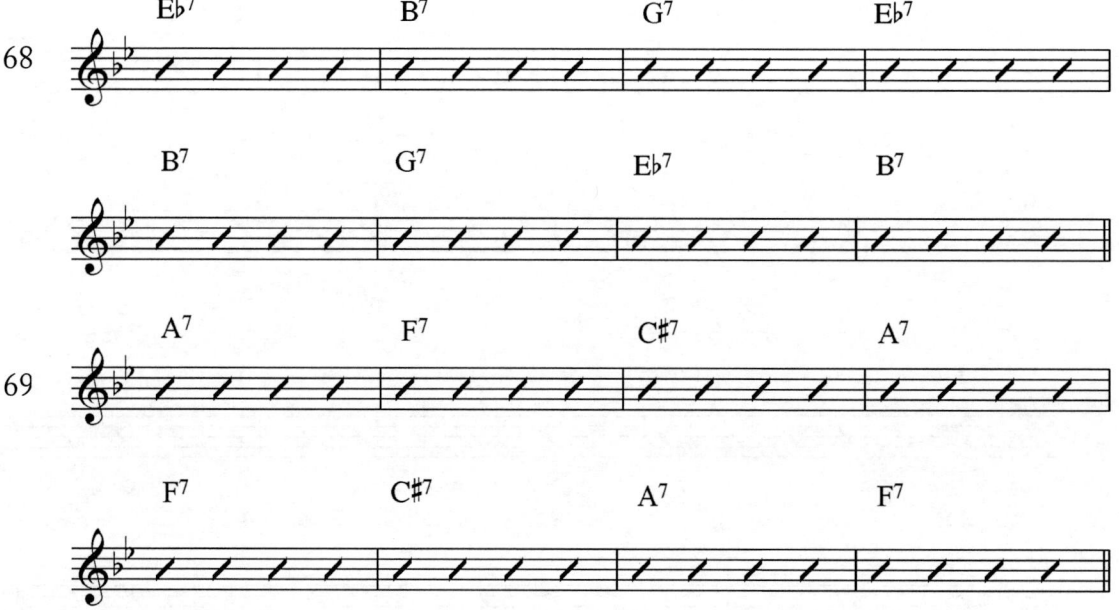

Ascending major thirds

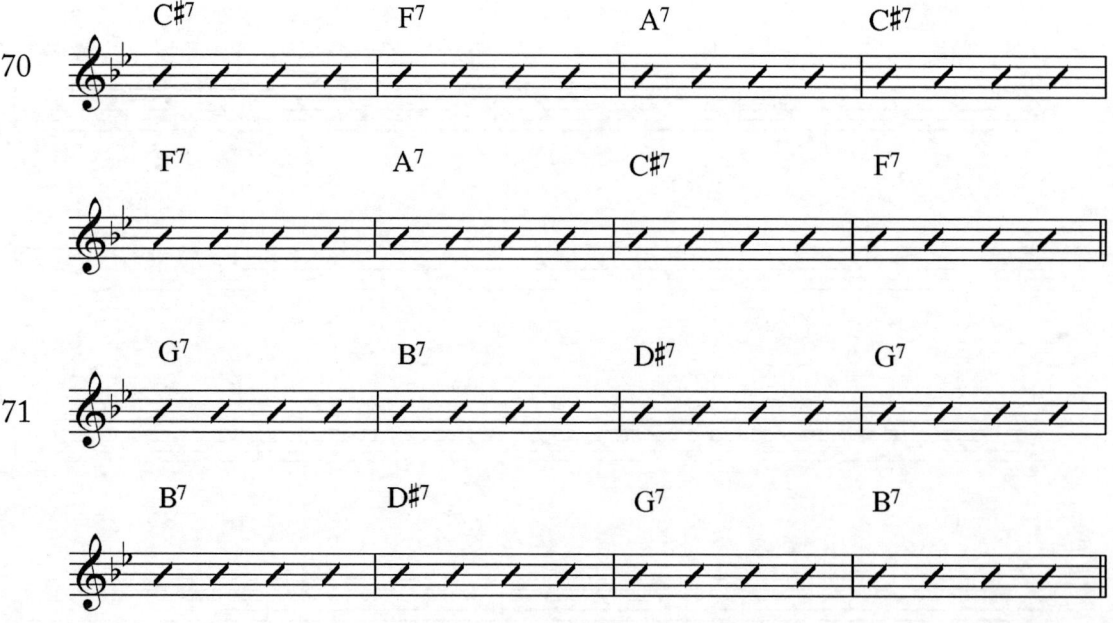

HARMONIC VARIATIONS OF THE BRIDGE (B SECTION)

(Playlist Tracks 72-77)

Bridge and Harmonic Variations

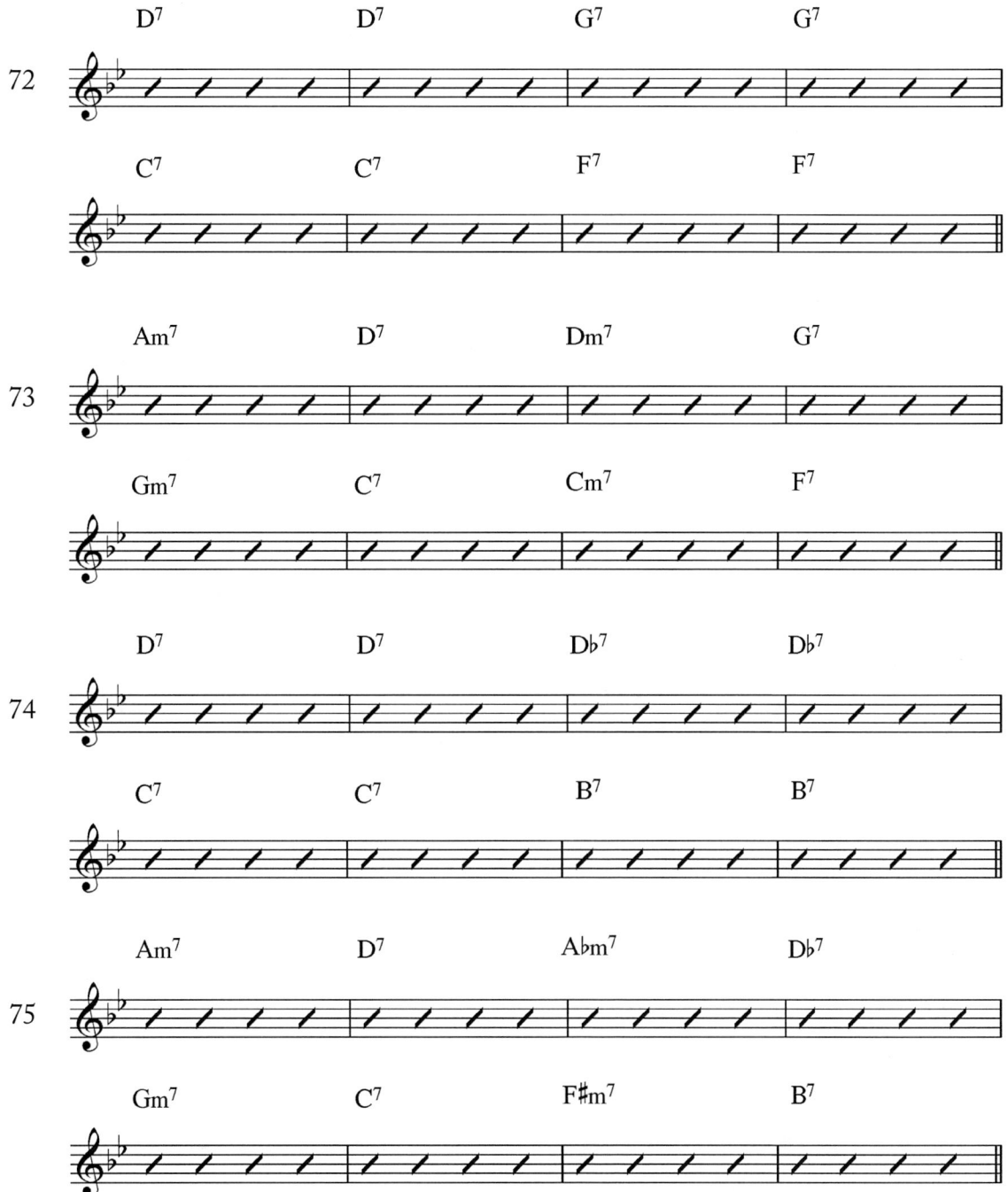

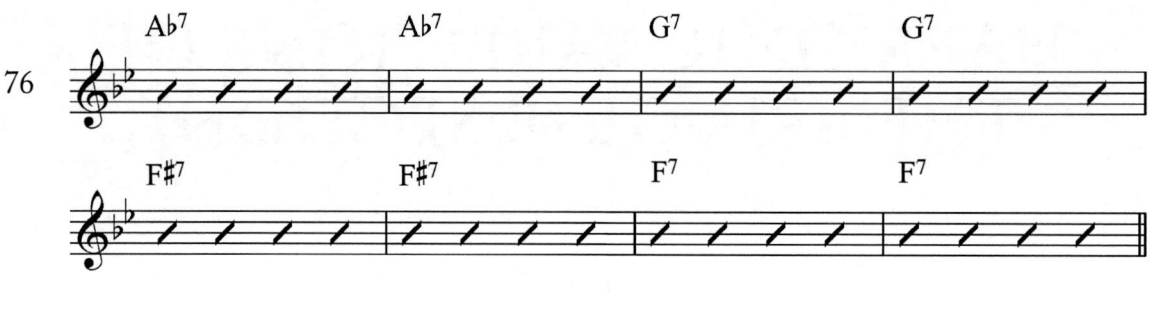

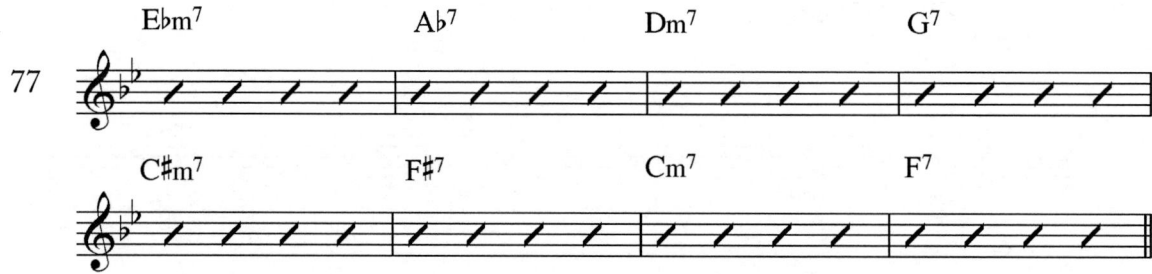

EXAMPLES FROM THE MASTERS: BRIDGE

Even though the standard harmonies of the bridge are generally used, there are sometimes deviations from the norm. In modern jazz alternative harmonies, it tends to be used more often.

- Dexter Gordon "Second Balcony Jump"

Gordon implies a set of chromatically descending ii-Vs in the first measure of the bridge.

- Michael Brecker "Anthropology"

Here Brecker also implies chromatically descending ii-Vs leading back into the last A section of the chorus.

- Charlie Parker "Anthropology"

Parker superimposes a set of ii-Vs in the first four measures of the bridge.

- Dexter Gordon "Red Cross"

Gordon states two chromatically descending melodies implying the displayed chords.

In contrafacts, the normal B section of rhythm changes has often been completely replaced with other harmonies while A sections are usually unchanged. Good examples of this are "Eternal Triangle," "Good Bait," "Nutty," "Room 608," or "CTA." John Coltrane's blues with a bridge "Locomotion" also features a harmonic variation of a rhythm changes bridge.

"Locomotion" and "CTA"

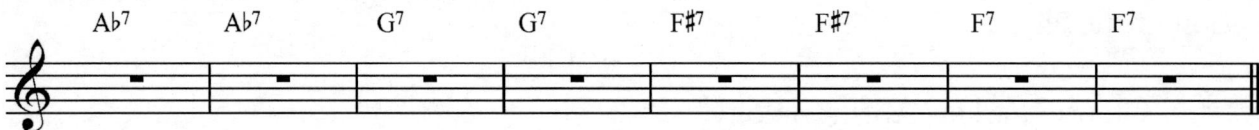

"Eternal Traingle" and "Straigt Ahead"

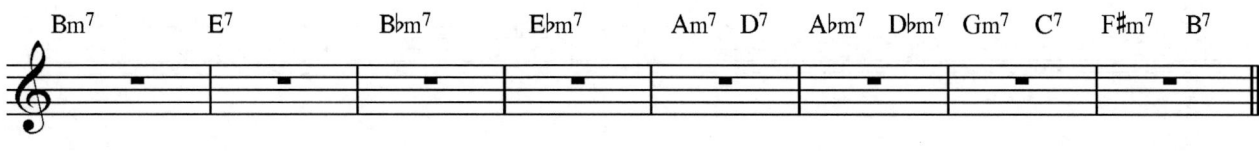

"Nutty"

"Good Bait"

"Room 608"

In his tune "Straight Ahead," composer/trumpeter Kenny Dorham used the same progression as in "Eternal Triangle" for the bridge.

In Thelonious Monk's "Nutty" and Tadd Dameron's "Good Bait," the bridges consist of a transposed version of the rhythm changes A section. The difference between "Nutty" and "Good Bait" revolves around the last two measures of each B section.

In "Room 608" Horace Silver moves to IV in the opening four measures of the bridge. Other tunes that go to IV in the B section are "Confirmation," "Move," "Night in Tunisia," "Alone Together," "Honeysuckle Rose," and many others.

TARGET NOTES AND GUIDE TONE LINES

There are several strategies that can be used to build a musical backbone for improvising. The following section demonstrates how you can come up with such backbones and how to use them in your own playing.

Generally, improvisers use passing tones, consonant skips, anticipations, suspensions, various types of neighbor notes, scales, arpeggios, and motives to fill the musical backbones we sometimes call "guide tone lines" or "target note lines."

REVIEW OF ORNAMENTAL NOTES

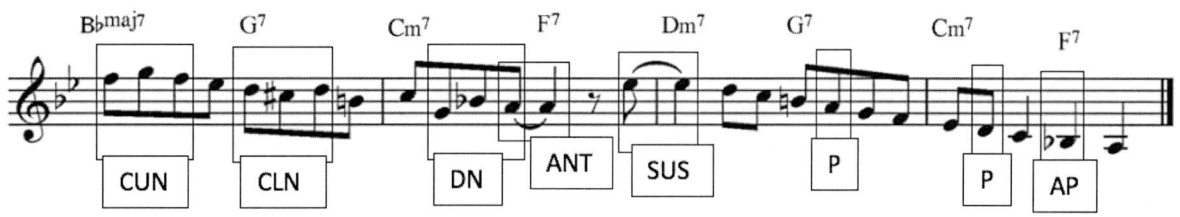

CUN = Complete upper neighbor
CLN = Complete lower neighbor
DN = Double neighbor
ANT = Anticipation
SUS = Suspension
P = Passing tone
AP = Accented passing tone

To practice these embellishments, you can begin by using them individually until you feel comfortable mixing two, three, and finally several different types of them.

USE OF ORNAMENTAL NOTES: EXAMPLES FROM THE MASTERS

- Sonny Rollins "Oleo"

Rollins plays a chord tone of each underlying chord on every first and third beat. Legendary performers never only chose a specific chord tone for their target tone lines but used a variety of chord tones. Here we mainly see the use of fifths and roots.

In the first measure Rollins uses an E as the upper neighbor to Dm which he plays on the third beat. He also approaches the same D with two half steps from below. He then plays a scale down to the G, which he plays on the first beat of the second measure. Rollins approaches the Eb of the second measure the same way he targets the D of the first measure.

- Don Byas "I Got Rhythm"

Byas mainly seems to focus on thirds at first but eventually switches to fifths. Analyze how Byas embellishes the target notes.

- Sonny Stitt "Eternal Triangle"

Stitt mainly bases his line on thirds. The second measure of the example includes a rhythmic displacement of a chord tone, which is caused by the use of upper neighbor 6. Analyze how Stitt embellishes the target notes.

Target notes do not always happen on strong beats (1 & 3) but sometimes also in other places.

Accented neighbor notes (see above), double neighbors, suspensions, or anticipations can shift the position of target notes.

- Don Byas "I Got Rhythm"

TARGET NOTE LINES CONSISTING OF THIRDS

Before being able to mix the different target pitches freely some preliminary exercises are necessary. In this example the target note line consists of every chord's third. The first two staffs display the plain target note line and the third and fourth staffs are an example of how it can be filled.

TARGET NOTE LINES CONSISTING OF FIFTHS

In this example the target note line consists of every chord's fifth. The first two staffs show the bare target note line, and the third and fourth staffs are an example of how it may be filled.

TARGET NOTE LINES CONSISTING OF SEVENTHS

In this example the target note line consists of every chord's seventh. The first two staffs display the plain target note line, and the third and fourth staffs are an example of how it can be filled.

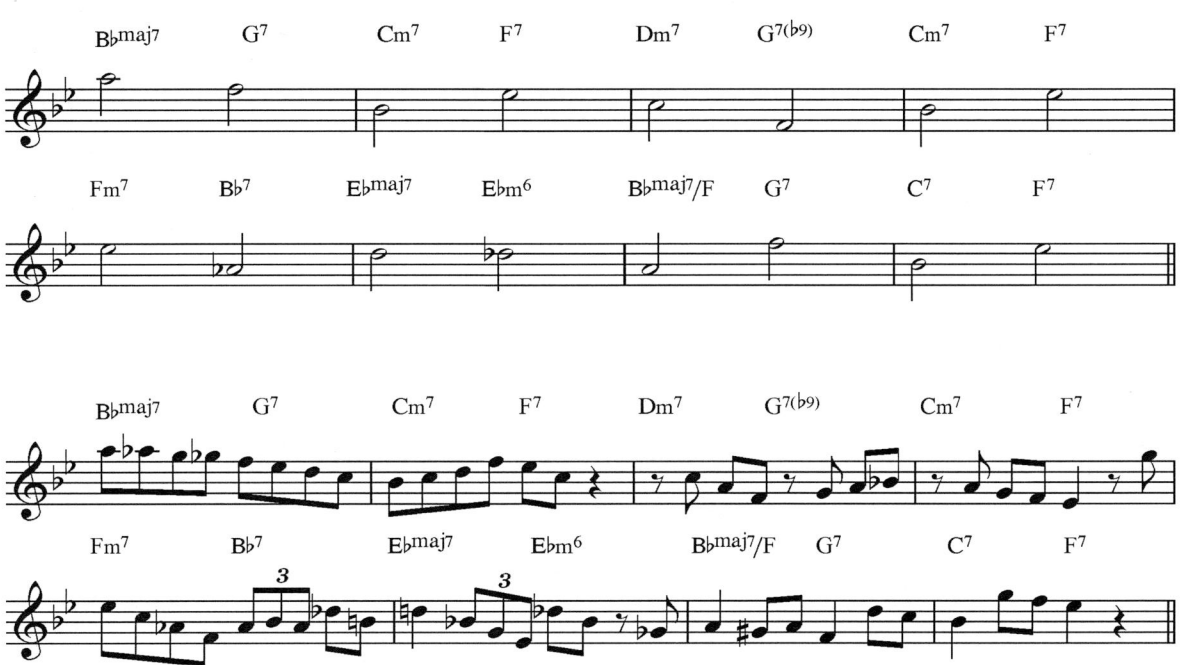

Use and Options of Chordal Extensions:

Besides using basic chord tones (1, 3, 5), you can also build target tone lines with extensions such as 9ths, 11ths and 13ths.

Major 7th chords:	9, #11, 13 (very rarely b13 – usually thought of as #5)
Dominant 7th chords:	b9, 9, #9, #11, b13, 13
Minor 7th chords:	9 (very rarely b9), 11, 13 (very rarely b13)
Minor 7th b5 chords:	9 (rarely b9), 11, b13
Dom. 7th sus 4:	9 (sometimes b9), 11, 13, (sometimes b13)

Major seventh and dominant seventh chords usually contain #11ths, while minor seventh chords have natural 11ths.

GUIDE TONE LINES

RULES FOR CONSTRUCTING GUIDE TONE LINES

1) Only use thirds and sevenths of all chords
2) Choose whether you want to begin with the third or seventh of the first chord
3) If you can, stay on the same pitch on the next chord
4) If you have to move, go to the closest third or seventh of the next chord
5) A minor third is usually the biggest interval a guide tone line includes in standard jazz harmony.

The following example shows a guide tone line and how it can be filled.

GUIDE TONE LINE FROM 3RD OF THE FIRST CHORD

This example is written over the A section of rhythm changes.

DIATONIC PLAYING

GUIDE TONE LINES WITH A SCHENKERIAN APPROACH

SCHENKER AND HIS PERSPECTIVE

Heinrich Schenker (1868-1935) was a music theorist, composer, teacher, and critic. He studied in Vienna with notable composers like Anton Bruckner (1824-1896) and is widely considered the leading theorist of tonal music in the twentieth century.

Rather than focusing on chord-to-chord voice leading (which Schenker also cared about) as in guide tone lines, a Schenkerian approach is concerned with voice leading at higher levels.

Examples:

Chord-to-chord voice leading: Getting from Dm^7 to G^7 in a ii-V progression

Schenkerian Approach: Getting from the fifth of a key to the root of the same key across an A section, chorus, or an entire solo.

Schenkerian lines are extended melodies that run from the third or the fifth of the key down to the root over the course of a section, a chorus, or even an entire solo. These long melodies happen on the musical background and middle ground levels and are usually filled on the foreground level. Most of tonal music works this way. Just like guide tone lines and target note lines, Schenkerian lines can help us to create a musical backbone that we can fill.

Schenkerian lines are an effective tool for playing rhythm changes diatonically but can also be used for chromatic improvisation. While there are several methods for organizing a diatonic approach to playing rhythm changes, being mindful of an overarching melodic structure is always helpful. Schenkerian lines are such structures.

HOW TO READ THE GRAPHS & EXAMPLES

- Some notes are more important than others. Neighbor notes or passing tones embellish more important notes
- Hollow note heads represent the most important notes
- Dotted slurs show prolonged notes
- Solid slurs show stepwise lines or consonant skips leading to or from an important note
- The tallest beam connects the notes with the highest importance
- Lower beamed lines show lesser importance and generally originate from or lead to a more significant pitch.

DID THE MASTERS REALLY KNOW THAT AND THINK LIKE THAT?

The artist's intention should not be considered the only or dominating measure according to which an artwork is interpreted or analyzed. In most cases is it impossible to know if improvisers were aware of concepts such as Schenker's.

Not everybody has the same amazing "gifts" the masters have. Concepts can be taught and learned but intuition is elusive and intangible. This leaves most of us with no choice but to practice concepts that help us to get closer to the music of the legends.

GUIDE LINE – SCHENKERIAN APPROACH

EXAMPLE 1 – SCHENKERIAN 5-DESCENT

In this example, F (the 5th of the key) is held in the first three measures at the background level. Then the key's 4 (Eb) is approached with an ascending scale. The line descends from D to C in the next two measures.

Like in a guide tone line, the material that fills the backbone consists of Ps, Ns, UNs, APs, scales, arpeggios, licks, etc.

The top staff shows the Schenkerian line (= melodic background structure) with graphic notation and the lower staff demonstrates how the foreground can be filled (= the solo). All examples are written over rhythm changes A sections.

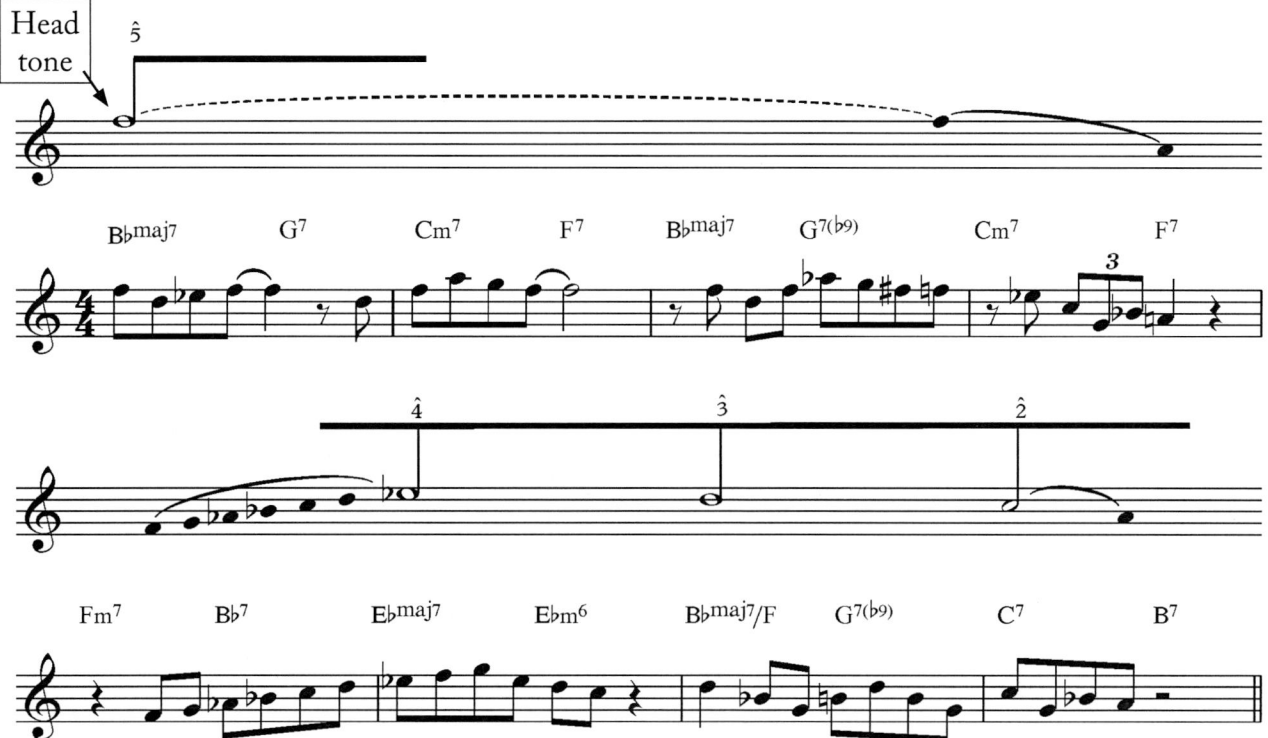

EXAMPLE 2 – SCHENKERIAN 5-DESCENT

Tonal music, like jazz, normally has a line that connects all the most important notes. Usually this most important line includes 5, 4, 3, 2, and 1 (or 3, 2, 1) of the key. Sometimes another line is added that occurs on the middle ground level.

These secondary lines always lead to or from a note that occurs in the most important line. The higher the beam, the more important the line. In example 2, two secondary lines originate from the head tone F.

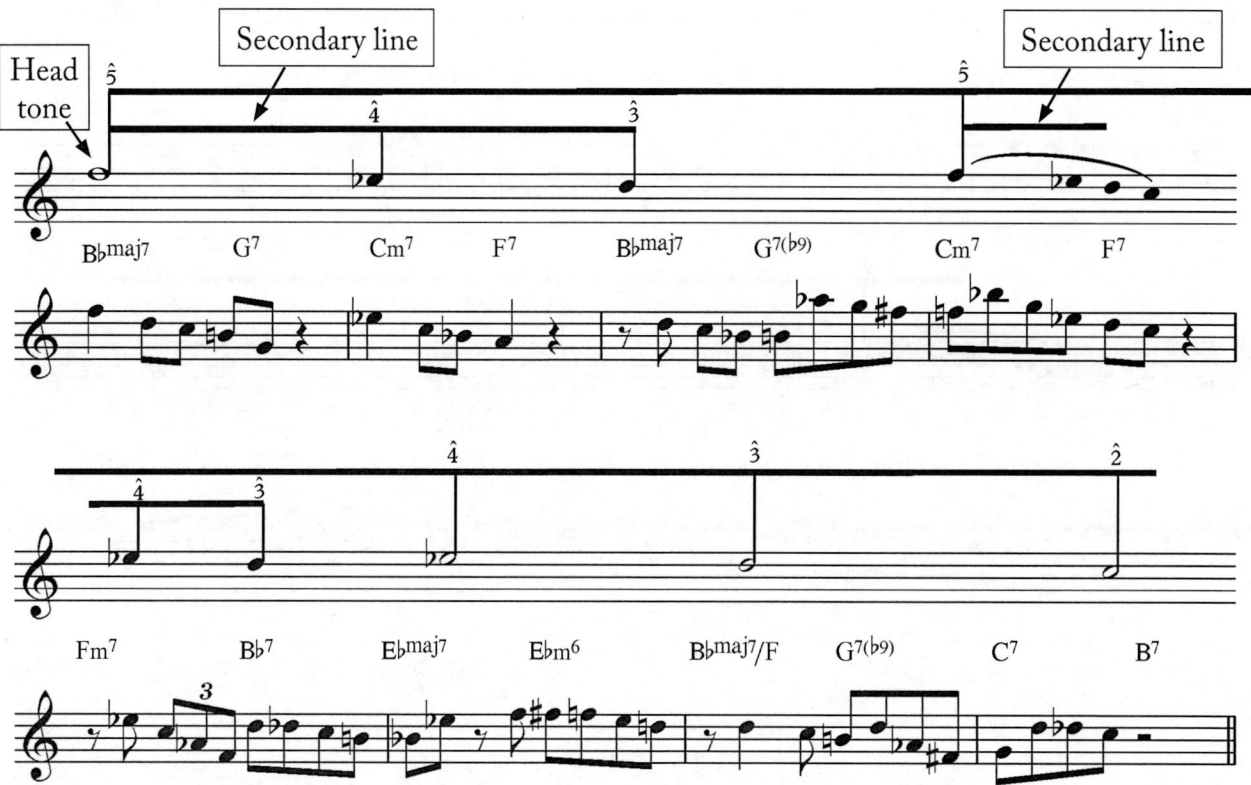

EXAMPLE 3 – SCHENKERIAN 5-DESCENT WITH INITIAL ASCENT

It is very common for the so-called *head tone* (=most important note) to be approached by an *initial* arpeggiated or *scalar ascent*. That's just an ascending scale/arpeggio or a part of a scale/arpeggio leading to the head tone. In example 3, an arpeggiation of the tonic triad and an upper neighbor leads to the *head tone* F. This example also includes a secondary line, which ends on the third and a primary line ending on the second scale degree.

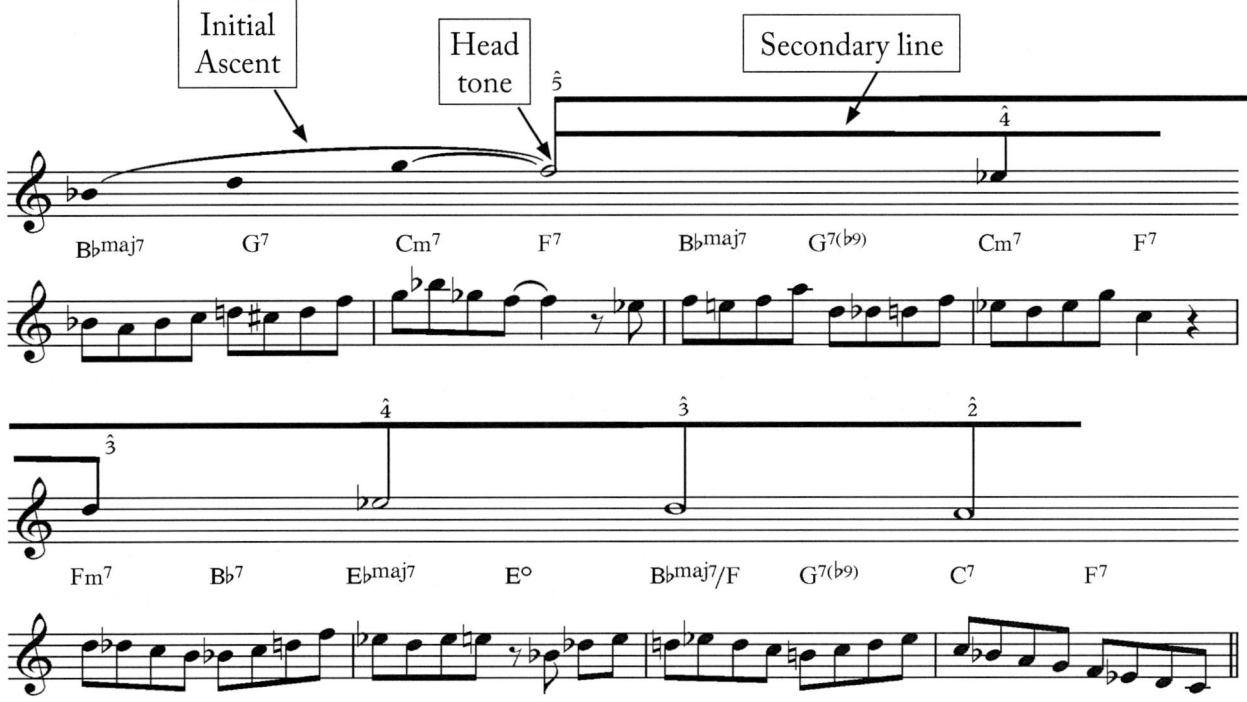

Some Terms

initial arpeggiated ascent	arpeggio leading to the head tone
initial scalar ascent	scale or scale fragment leading to the head tone
head tone	Most important note in the Schenkerian line

EXAMPLE 4 – SCHENKERIAN 3-DESCENT

In example 4, the third is the *head tone* of the main line. Notice how there can be non-diatonic pitches within the main line. In jazz, you will find that the succession 5, 4, 3, 2, 1 is often replaced by 5, 4, ♭3, 1.

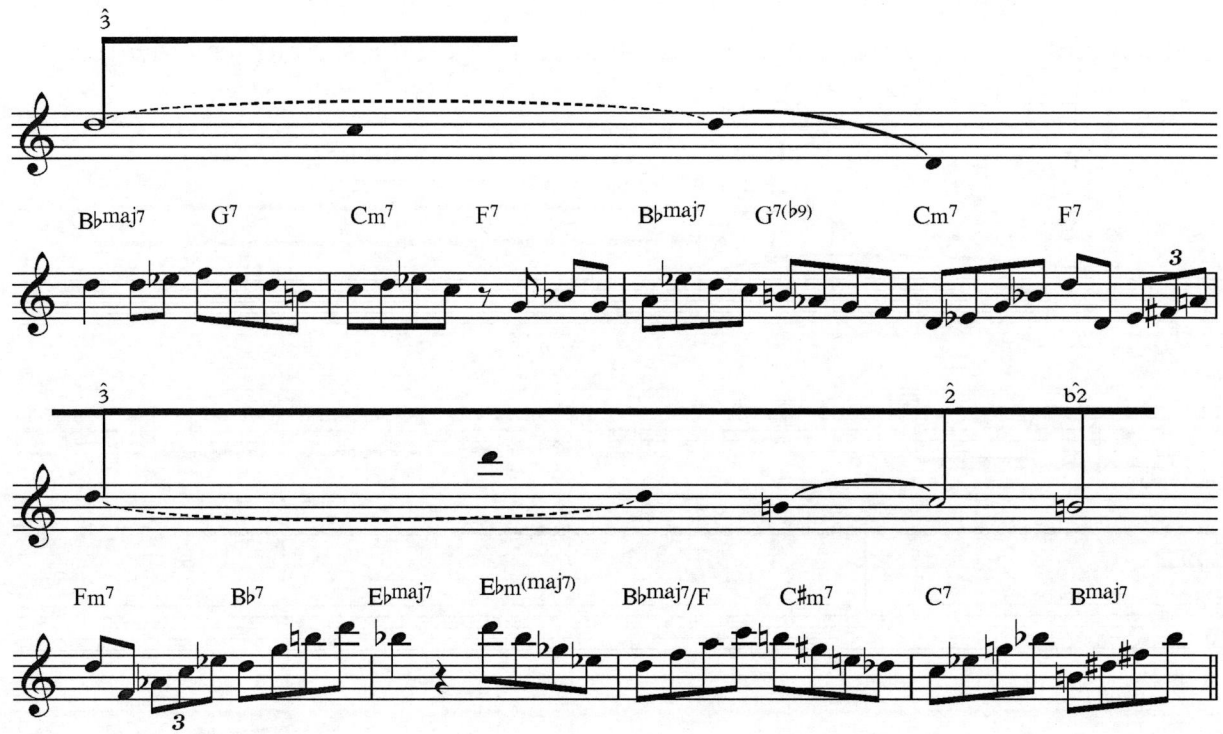

REGISTER TRANSFER & OCTAVE EQUIVALENCE

When improvising or composing with a Schenkerian approach, identical notes that are played in different octaves have the same function. In other words, the main descent does not need to happen within one register or octave. This is very useful when you get toward the end of your range while playing.

SCHENKERIAN LINES: EXAMPLES FROM THE MASTERS

- John Coltrane "Oleo" - second half of second A

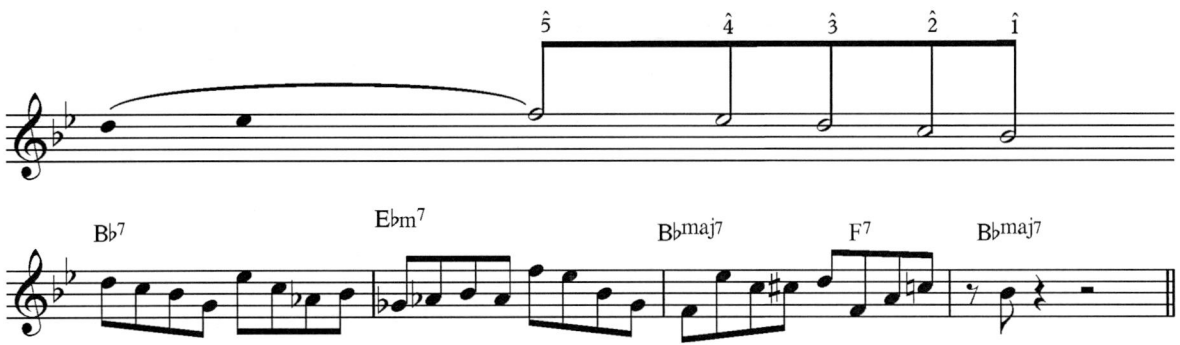

- John Coltrane "Oleo" - second half of second A

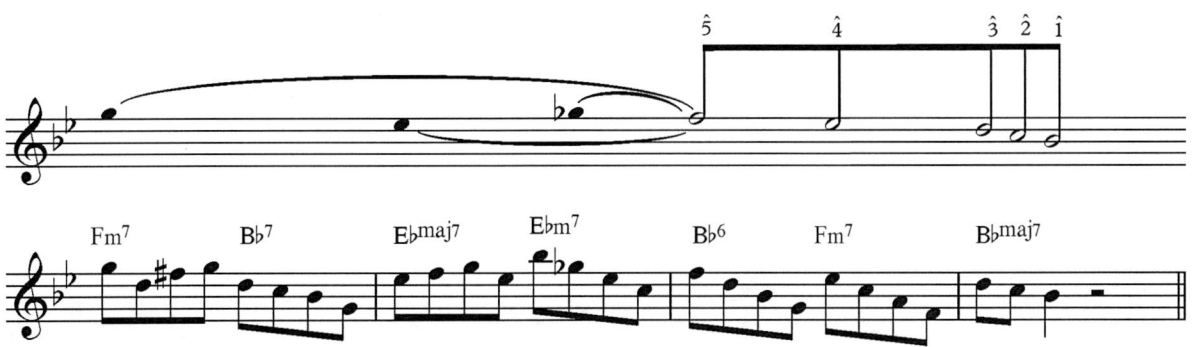

Both examples stem from the second half of the second A section of Coltrane's solo on "Oleo."

In both instances Coltrane works his way up to the *head tone*. In the first example the head tone is approached with a three progression (D, E♭, F), and in the second example with neighbor notes (G & G♭ from above and E♭ from below).

Notice how Coltrane jumps up a minor seventh in the third measure of the first example. It seems that he wanted to keep the structural line within the same octave.

- Sonny Stitt "Eternal Triangle" – second half of second A

This example shows how octave equivalence and register transfers happen in real playing situations. The line begins in one register, but Stitt drops the third (D) and ends in yet another register.

- Sonny Rollins "Eternal Triangle"

In Schenkerian theory seven can replace two. This is based on the perfect authentic cadences, which moves from 7-1 in the top voice. Rollins was probably not thinking about Cm^7 in the last measure, but rather extended $B\flat maj^7$.

OTHER DIATONIC TECHNIQUES

TRIADS

The tonic triad is the core of tonal music and diatonic playing. It is necessary to practice ways of embellishing this fundamental musical building block. It is crucial to be aware of the underlying background and middle ground harmonies when improvising diatonically.

EMBELLISHING TRIADS: EXAMPLES FROM THE MASTERS

- Sonny Stitt "Eternal Triangle"

In this example Stitt uses the key's tonic triad throughout the first four measures of the A section. Here he is using an approach that relies on the background perspective, since all four measures are based on the I chord.

- Dexter Gordon "Red Cross"

Gordon also embellishes the tonic triad in this example. He approaches each note of the triad with a half step from below. The background perspective is also used here.

- Dexter Gordon "Red Cross"

Gordon also ornaments the tonic triad in this example. Each chord tone is approached with a three-note group.

- Cannonball Adderley "Oleo"

This embellishment only ornaments the root and fifth of the tonic triad, but a 3/4 cross rhythm is also implied.

- John Coltrane "Good Bait"

Here Coltrane performs an embellishment of the ii^7 chord. In contrast to the earlier examples, it is not the I chord which is prolonged but the predominant chord Cm^7.

TRIADIC EMBELLISHMENTS: EXERCISES DERIVED FROM THE MASTERS

All the derived exercises are transposed to the key of C but should be practiced in all keys.

There are countless other ways to ornament triads and seventh chords besides what is displayed in these examples. The following exercises are also derived from the jazz tradition.

1)

CMa7

2)

CMa7

3)

CMa7

4)

CMa7

5)

CMa7

SEQUENCES: EXAMPLES FROM THE MASTERS

Sequences are very effective for expressing middle ground and foreground harmonies. Often diatonic sequences are hidden by ornamental pitches, but sometimes they are more obvious.

- Sonny Stitt "Eternal Triangle"

Stitt uses the three diatonic triads B♭maj – Cmin – Dmin in sequence.

- Dexter Gordon "Second Balcony Jump"

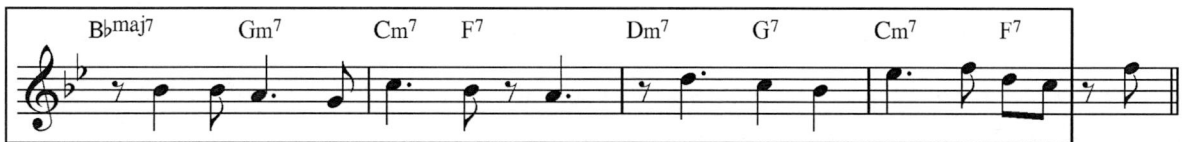

Gordon quotes Richard Rodgers' and Lorenz Hart's "My Heart Stood Still," which is an ascending sequence.

- John Coltrane "Oleo"

This example features a diatonic third pattern played in sequence.

- Dexter Gordon "Red Cross"

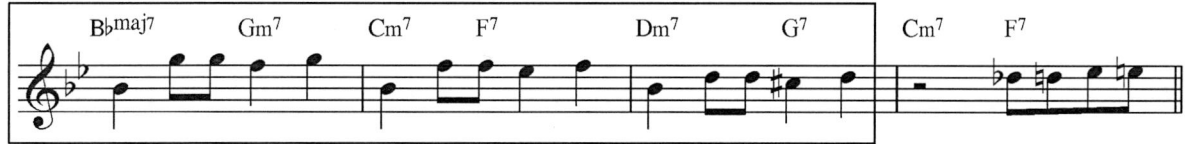

Here Gordon plays a descending sequence with a B♭ pedal tone.

SEQUENCE EXERCISES

These exercises represent some ideas that illustrate how sequences can be used when playing rhythm changes. The exercises should be practiced with varied rhythms and in different keys. Shifting a sequence back or forth an eighth note can make a world of a difference.

USE OF THE BLUES SCALE: EXAMPLES FROM THE MASTERS

Sometimes performers use the minor blues scale for the A sections of rhythm changes.[*] Foreground harmonies are included in the following examples to how the progression is overridden by the blues statements.

Mostly players use the blues scale that is built on the root but, you can also use the blues scale that is built on the sixth degree of the key.

- Sonny Stitt "Eternal Triangle"

- Sonny Rollins "Eternal Triangle"

- Michael Brecker "Moose The Mooch"

- Dexter Gordon "Second Balcony Jump"

---

[*] For a comprehensive discussion of the minor and major blues scales and their historical and practical applications see Dan Greenblatt's book *The Blues Scales* (Petaluma, CA.: Sher Music. Inc., 2004)

PENTATONIC SCALES

Besides using blues scales, pentatonic scales are also very useful. The A sections of the melody of "I Got Rhythm" largely consists of a Bb major pentatonic. Pentatonic scales can consist of any five pitches, which makes 9th chords great sources for pentatonics. (E.g.: C^9 = C, E, G, Bb, D; as a pentatonic = Bb, C, D, E, G)

Some options for the use of pentatonic scales over rhythm changes:

Background level A section:

- Bbmaj/Gmin
- Fmaj/Dmin
- Bbmaj^9 chord pent: A, Bb, C, D, F
- Bbmin/Dbmaj (Bluesy sound)

Middle ground level Bridge:

Chromatically descending pentatonics are an effective way to play over the bridge.

Option 1

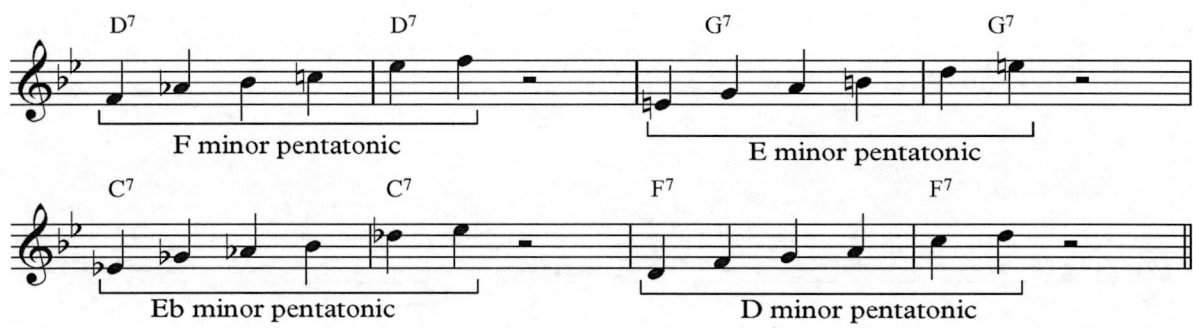

Option 2

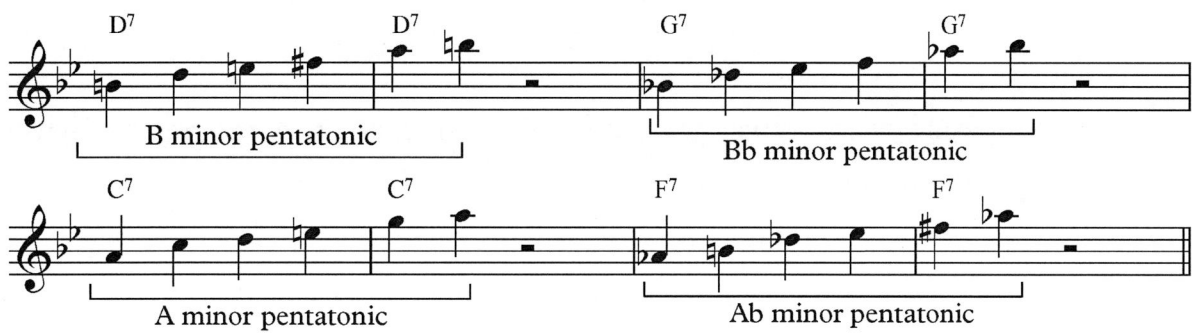

In order to make your pentatonic playing more coherent, you can use guidelines.

In the following example, option 2 is the foundation. The top two staffs are a stepwise guideline and the bottom two staffs demonstrate how the line can be filled.

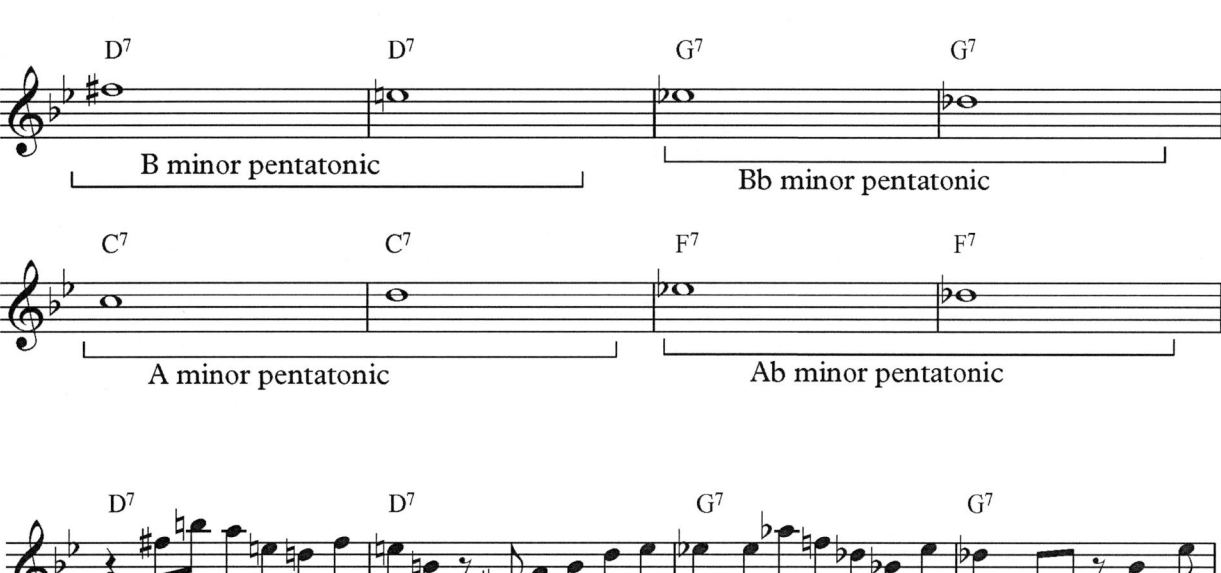

ETUDES

- Etudes 1-7 are written over the common rhythm changes progression without harmonic variations
- The etudes are arranged in increasing order of difficulty and complexity.
- The tempo markings are baselines. You should start slowly and make sure you can play them without mistakes before increasing the tempo.
- Follow the articulations

ETUDE 1 "FIVE"

The entire first etude is strictly constructed of pitches from the Bb pentatonic scale.

ETUDE 2 "COMMON GROUND"

The melodic and rhythmic statements in "Common Ground" are relatively simple, which makes is easier to get comfortable with the song.

The first four measures feature an ascending melodic sequence, which is followed by a shorter descending sequence.

First four measures of the second A section are composed as a musical period (= basic idea, contrasting idea, basic idea, contrasting idea). The basic idea is a repeated Bb stated as quarter notes.

Notice the recurring A in the bridge, which is stated over every chord. Common tones are a great way to restrict yourself and explore how the same note sounds over different harmonies.

Jazz lovers might recognize the rhythmic figure in the beginning of the last A section. When quoting you don't always have to state the original melody verbatim. You can also just use the rhythm and add your own pitches.

ETUDE 3 "FOUR"

The interval of a perfect fourth serves as the main compositional idea in this etude. Restricting yourself to an interval in your own writing and improvisations can be very rewarding.

ETUDE 4 "COMBINATION"

In "Combination" all A sections follow a Schenkerian approach in regard to large scale voice leading.

The bridge features a melodic idea that is repeated. The roots of the underlying dominant play an important role within the bridge.

ETUDE 5 "FOLLOW THE LINE"

In "Follow The Line," all A sections follow a Schenkerian approach. In the bridge the Dominant$^{7(\#11)}$ sound is explored.

ETUDE 6 "BIG PICTURE"

In "Big Picture," the first A sections follows a Schenkerian approach while the second A section features use of the Bb minor blues scale.

In the bridge one phrase is transposed several times to fit the underlying chords. Slight rhythmic variations help to make the transposed restatements less obvious.

ETUDE 7 "UPSIDE DOWN"

The compositional material is based on chromatic voice leading in combination with the use of triads. Sixths are identical to thirds by inversion. This fact is explored in "Upside Down" as well.

ETUDE 8 "OPTIONS"

"Options" features bebop chord progressions with slight harmonic variations and includes melodic devices from Dexter Gordon, Michael Brecker, John Coltrane, and Charlie Parker.

ETUDE 9 "CHICAGO"

Like "Options," this etude features relatively common, yet important, harmonic progressions and slight variations thereof. There are some challenging large intervallic jumps and harmonic variants that will keep you on your toes. "Chicago" includes melodic devices from Chris Potter, Michael Brecker, and Bill Evans.

ETUDE 10 "BIG BIRD"

"Big Bird" includes melodic devices from Charlie Parker, Eric Alexander, John Coltrane, Michael Brecker, and Sonny Stitt. Besides bebop-related vocabulary, this etude presents material from the blues vernacular. The bridge features a substitution that is used by some advanced improvisers.

ETUDE 11 "FOR VIC"

"For Vic" includes melodic devices from Stan Getz, Joe Henderson, Paul Desmond, John Coltrane, and Sonny Stitt. It is dedicated to the great jazz guitarist Vic Juris.

ETUDE 12 "EXCURSION"

"Excursion" includes melodic devices from Dexter Gordon, Michael Brecker, Joel Frahm, Charlie Parker, Eddie Harris, and John Coltrane. This etude demonstrates a few ways that you can use to step out of the conventional harmonic context for a moment.

ETUDE 13 "STEPPIN' DOWN"

"Steppin' Down" explores the idea of a descending melodic and/or harmonic direction throughout the first two A sections. "Steppin' Down" includes melodic devices from Sonny Stitt, and John Coltrane, Phineas Newborn, and others.

ETUDE 14 "MIRROR IMAGE"

"Mirror Image" utilizes the concept of musical symmetry. Accordingly, you'll find augmented scale patterns, tritone substitutions, and chromatically descending ideas at play here. "Excursion" includes melodic devices from Eddie Harris, Dexter Gordon, and John Coltrane.

ETUDE 15 "EXPRESS TRAIN"

"Express Train" includes melodic devices from John Coltrane, Joel Frahm, Stan Getz, and Michael Brecker. Harmonically this etude is inspired by Coltrane's contributions, which are heard on albums such as *Giant Steps*. Observe how Coltrane's changes can be integrated within rhythm changes.

ETUDE 16 "BIG RED"

"Big Red" is based on a harmonic substitution that I first heard from Eric Alexander. It also includes melodic ideas from Eddie Harris, Dexter Gordon, and John Coltrane. The central harmonic idea consists of ascending half steps.

ETUDE 17 "THE PATRON"

"The Patron" is inspired by Don Byas' playing but also includes material from Dexter Gordon and Eddie Harris. This chromatic progression is essentially a variant of the well-known circle of fourths superimposition which is also frequently used by advanced improvisers over rhythm changes. Transpose every other chord in the chromatic sequence up/down a tritone and write your own etudes and exercises over the resulting progression. The next etude can be seen as an example of this suggested exercise.

ETUDE 18 "TRIAL AND ERROR"

"Trial and Error" features the famous circle of fifths progression as it is commonly applied to the A sections as a substitution. Moreover, this etude features the melodic 1,2,3,5 patterns which were made famous by John Coltrane. This short four-note pattern is an extremely effective tool for outlining harmony in a short period of time. There are 24 ways of reconfiguring this four-note pattern. All resulting permutations sound slightly different. Many advanced improvisers have practiced these permutations.

Here are all 24 of them:

1235	2135	3215	5123
1253	2153	3251	5132
1325	2351	3125	5231
1352	2315	3152	5213
1532	2513	3512	5312
1523	2531	3521	5321

ETUDE 19 "CHOICES"

"Choices" employs ideas based on hexatonic scales as well as the bebop language, and the diminished scale.

ETUDE 20 "LITTLE BIRD"

"Little Bird" utilizes the progression of "C.T.A." which is based on the idea of descending whole steps. It also revolves around the interval of a 4th from a melodic perspective. The Last A section demonstrates how triads can be employed in open position coupled with an underlying 12/8 feel. "C.T.A." was written by saxophonist Jimmy Heath and "Little Bird" was his nickname.

THE RHYTHM CHANGES GUIDE

"Four"

THE RHYTHM CHANGES GUIDE
"Follow The Line"

LUKAS GABRIC

"Options"

★ = suggested final note of the chorus - ignore if you choose to play several choruses in sequence

THE RHYTHM CHANGES GUIDE
"Chicago"

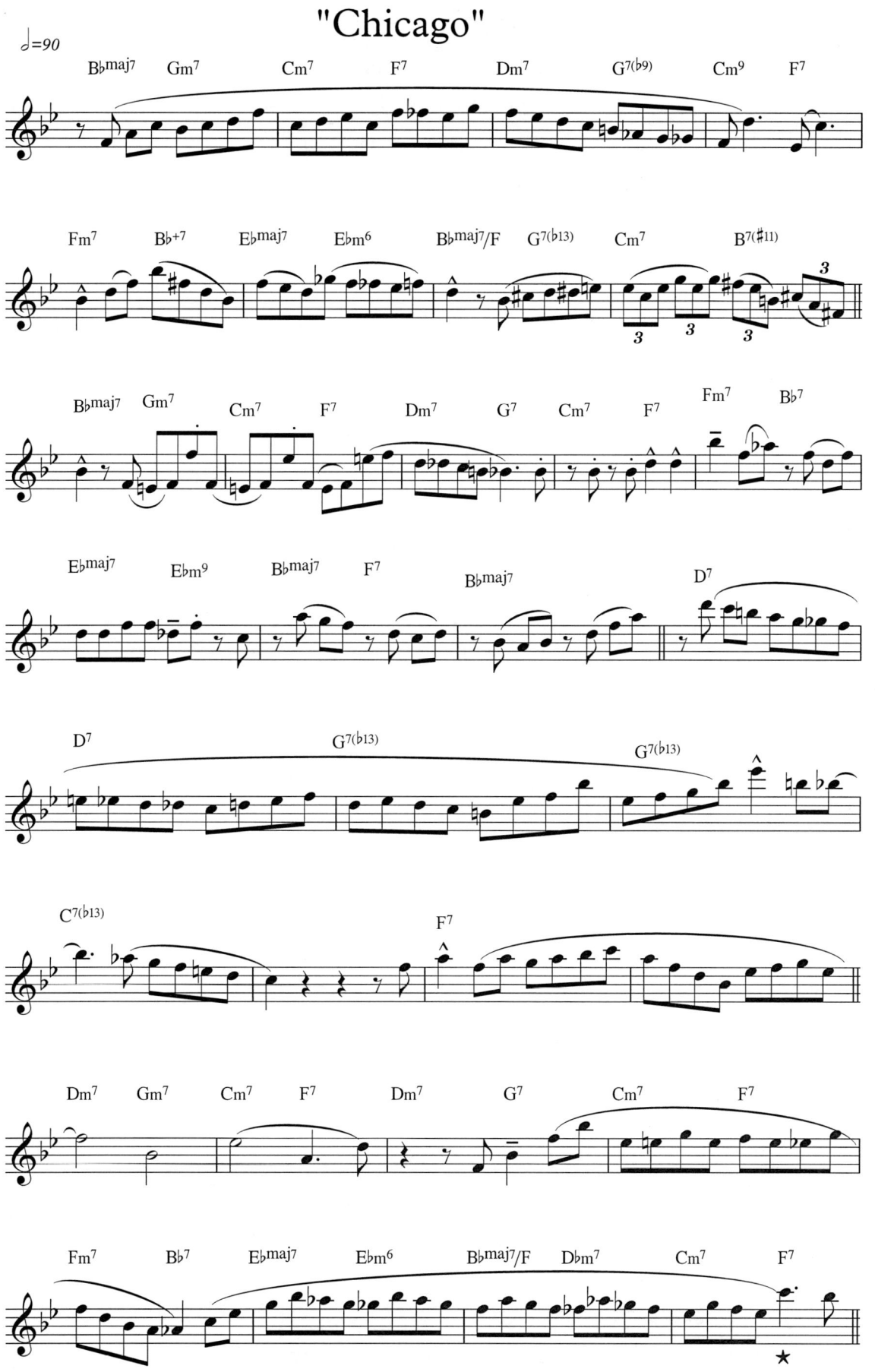

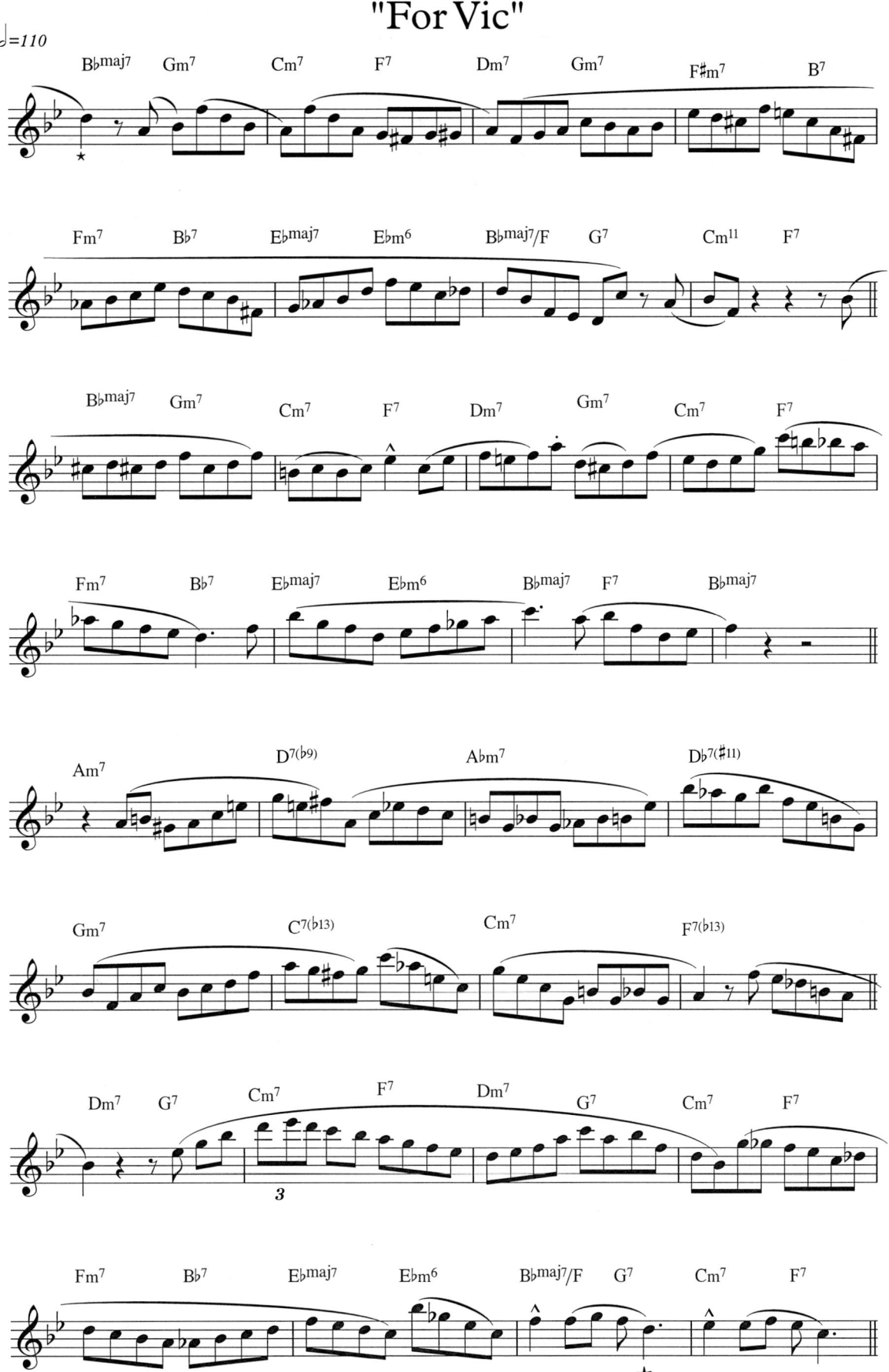

LUKAS GABRIC

"Excursion"

THE RHYTHM CHANGES GUIDE

"Steppin' Down"

THE RHYTHM CHANGES GUIDE

"Express Train"

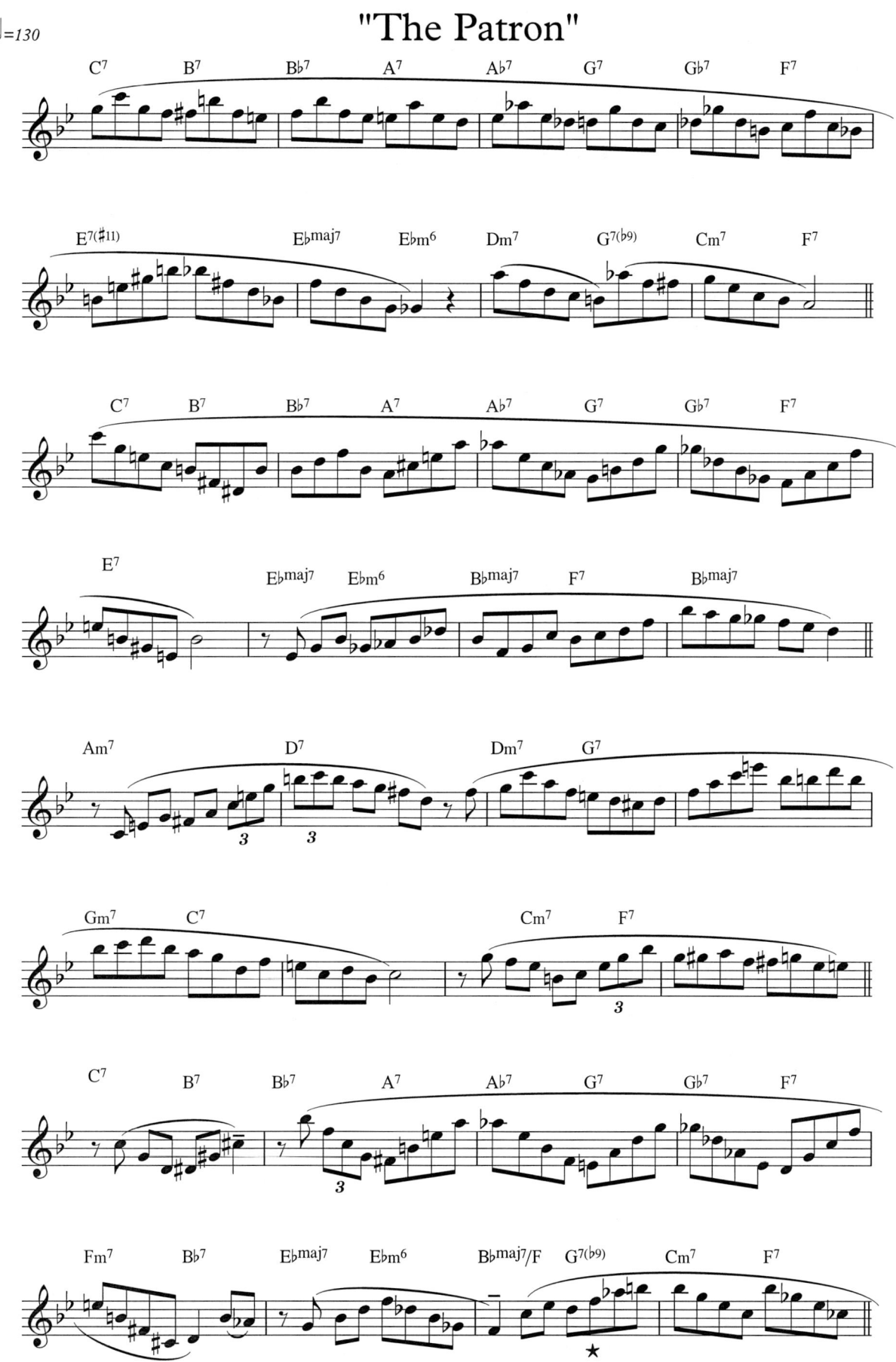

LUKAS GABRIC

"Trial and Error"

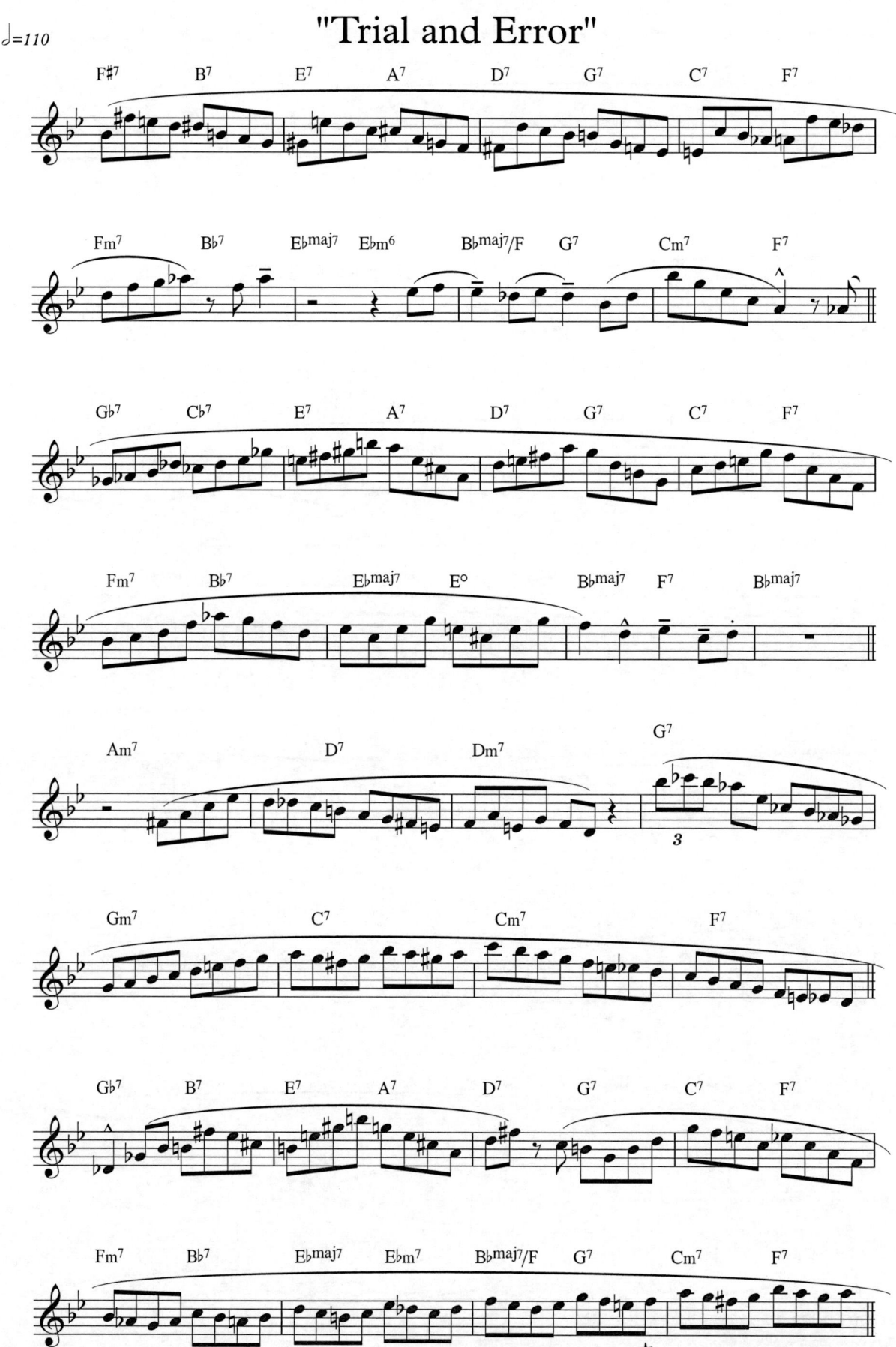

"Choices"

RECORDINGS

Dexter Gordon, *Stable Mable* (LP), Steeplechase SCS-1040, Denmark 1975

Gillespie, Rollins, Stitt, *Sonny Side Up* (LP, Album, Mono), Verve Records MG V-8262, US 1959

Will Lee, Birdhouse, Skip Records GmbH, 2001

The Miles Davis Sextet, *Jazz At The Plaza Vol. 1* (LP, Album), Columbia C 32470, US 1973

Dexter Gordon, *Go!* (LP, Album, Mono), Blue Note BLP 4112, US 1962

Mel Lewis, *Mel Lewis And Friends* (LP, Album, Gat), A&M Records SP-716, US 1977

Hank Mobley, Al Cohn, John Coltrane, Zoot Sims, *Tenor Conclave* (LP, Album, Mono) Prestige PRLP 7074, US   1957

Don Byas, *Anthropology* (CD, Comp, RE), Jazz Colours 874774-2, Germany 2003

Don Byas, "Indiana," "I Got Rhythm" *Town Hall Concert, 1945*, Atlantic – SD 2 – 310, US 1973

Miles Davis, *Relaxin' With The Miles Davis Quintet* (LP, Album, Mono, 1st), Prestige PRLP 7129, US 1958

Charlie Parker, *Thriving from a Riff*. The Be Bop Boys. Savoy Records. 1945. 903-B.

Miles Davis, *Relaxin' With The Miles Davis Quintet* (LP, Album, Mono, 1st), Prestige PRLP 7129, US 1958

Horace Silver, *Horace Silver And The Jazz Messengers* (LP, Comp, Mono, Lex), Blue Note BLP 1518, US 1956

Miles Davis, *Miles* (LP, Album, Mono), Prestige LP 7014, PRLP 7014, US 1956

Miles Davis, *Bags Groove* (LP, Comp, Mono)Prestige 7109, US 1957

John Coltrane, *Soultrane* (LP, Album, Mono)Prestige, Prestige 7142, PRLP 7142, US 1958

SHER MUSIC CO.
The World's Premier Jazz & Latin Music Book Publisher!

BEST-SELLING BOOKS BY MARK LEVINE
The Jazz Theory Book
The Jazz Piano Book
Jazz Piano Masterclass: The Drop 2 Book
How to Voice Standards at the Piano

THE WORLD'S BEST FAKE BOOKS
The New Real Book - Vol.1 - C, Bb and Eb
The New Real Book - Vol.2 - C, Bb and
The New Real Book - Vol.3 - C, Bb, Eb and Bass Clef
The Real Easy Book - Vol.1 - C, Bb, Eb and Bass Clef (Three-Horn Edition)
The Real Easy Book - Vol.2 - C, Bb, Eb and Bass Clef
The Real Easy Book - Vol.3 - C, Bb, Eb and Bass Clef
The Latin Real Easy Book - C, Bb, Eb and Bass Clef
The Standards Real Book - C, Bb and Eb
The Latin Real Book - C, Bb and Eb
The Real Cool Book - 14 West Coast 'Cool' Jazz Octet Charts
The All-Jazz Real Book - C, Bb and Eb
The European Real Book - C, Bb and Eb
The Best of Sher Music Real Books - C, Bb and Eb
The World's Greatest Fake Book - C version only
The Yellowjackets Songbook - (all parts)
The Latin Real Book - C, Bb and Eb

DIGITAL FAKE BOOKS (at shermusic.com only)
The New Real Book - Vol.1 - C, Bb and Eb
The Digital Standards Songbook
The Digital Real Book

LATIN MUSIC BOOKS
Decoding Afro-Cuban Jazz: The Music of Chucho Valdés and Irakere - by Chucho Valdés and Rebeca Mauleón
The Salsa Guidebook - by Rebeca Mauleón
The Latin Real Easy Book - C, Bb, Eb and Bass Clef
The Latin Bass Book - by Oscar Stagnaro and Chuck Sher
The True Cuban Bass - by Carlos del Puerto and Silvio Vergara
The Brazilian Guitar Book - by Nelson Faria
Inside the Brazilian Rhythm Section - Nelon Faria/Cliff Korman
The Conga Drummer's Guidebook - by Michael Spiro
Language of the Masters - by Michael Spiro
Introduction to the Conga Drum DVD - by Michael Spiro
Afro-Caribbean Grooves for Drumset - by Jean-Philippe Fanfant
Afro-Peruvian Percussion Ensemble - by Hector Morales
Flamenco Improvisation, Vol. 1-3 - by Enrique Vargas

Bilingual
The Latin Real Book - C, Bb and Eb
101 Montunos - by Rebeca Mauleón
Muy Caliente! - Afro-Cuban Book Play-Along CD

Libros en Español
El Libro del Jazz Piano - by Mark Levine
Teoria del Jazz - by Mark Levine (digital only)

JAZZ METHOD BOOKS
The Improvisor's Bass Method - by Chuck Sher
Concepts for Bass Soloing - by Marc Johnson & Chuck Sher
Walking Bassics - by Ed Fuqua
Foundation Exercises for Bass - by Chuck Sher

GUITAR
Jazz Guitar Voicings: The Drop 2 Book - by Randy Vincent
Three-Note Voicings and Beyond - by Randy Vincent
Line Games - by Randy Vincent
Jazz Guitar Soloing: The Cellular Approach - by Randy Vincent
The Guitarist's Introduction to Jazz - by Randy Vincent

PIANO
Playing for Singers - by Mike Greensill
An Approach to Comping: The Essentials - by Jeb Patton
An Approach to Comping, Vol.2: Advanced - by Jeb Patton
Wisdom of the Hand - by Marius Nordal

OTHER INSTRUMENTS
Inner Drumming - by George Marsh
Method for Chromatic Harmonica - by Max de Aloe
Modern Etudes for Solo Trumpet - by Cameron Pearce
New Orleans Trumpet - by Jim Thornton

FOR ALL INSTRUMENTS
The Jazz Harmony Book - by David Berkman
The Jazz Musician's Guide to Creative Practicing - D. Berkman
The Jazz Singer's Guidebook - by David Berkman
Metaphors for the Musician - Randy Halberstadt
Forward Motion - by Hal Galper
The Serious Jazz Practice Book - by Barry Finnerty
The Serious Jazz Book II - by Barry Finnerty
Building Solo Lines From Cells - by Randy Vincent
The Real Easy Ear Training Book - by Roberta Radley
Reading, Writing and Rhythmetic - by Roberta Radley
Minor is Major - by Dan Greenblatt
Jazz Scores and Analysis - Vol.1 - by Rick Lawn
Essential Grooves - by Moretti, Nicholl and Stagnaro
The Jazz Solos of Chick Corea - transcribed by Peter Sprague

FOR STUDENT MUSICIANS
The Blues Scales - by Dan Greenblatt - C, Bb and Eb
Rhythm First! - by Tom Kamp - C, Bb, Eb and Bass Clef
The Guitarist's Introduction to Jazz - by Randy Vincent
Jazz Songs for Student Violinists - by Keefe and Mitchell

CDs
Poetry+Jazz: A Magical Marriage
The New Real Book Play-Along CDs (for Vol.1) - #1, 2 and 3
The Latin Real Book Sampler CD
The Music of Charles Stevens

ALL METHOD BOOKS ALSO AVAILABLE IN DIGITAL FORM ONLINE

For more info, see SherMusic.com